"You may not know Colin Creel, [...] in for a treat. If you're old enough [...] haven't celebrated your thirtieth birthday, Colin is going to give you some sound wisdom about these very, very important years. Since time travel is still under development, you're not going to get to do these years over again. Lucky for you, you've picked up this book, and your new friend, Colin, is going to give you some great perspectives on these fantastic years."

—**ROBERT WOLGEMUTH**, author, *The Most Important Place on Earth*

"*Perspectives* is a book that spurs you on in your walk with Christ. Like a good guidebook, Colin Creel offers insight into some of the critical moments on the journey through ones 20s. He has woven together the advice of many sages—ancient and contemporary, tying in 'seasoned advice' from real people who have been on that road before and honestly tying it to his own experience— all in a hope to make the journey a little bit better for those who come after him. His thirty meditations tackle issues, offer insight, and ask questions. I highly recommend this book—and the reading list one accumulates as you move through it. *Perspectives* will help make that journey a richer experience as the reader navigates the pivotal years of the third decade of life—and beyond."

—**EVAN HUNTER**, director, Ivy Jungle Network

"*Perspectives* is a smart resource for anyone who wants to succeed in their relationships, career, and walk with God during their twenties—and beyond."

—TARA DAWN CHRISTENSEN, Miss America 1997, speaker and singer

"As someone who works closely with college students, I wholeheartedly believe that *Perspectives* should be required reading for all twentysomethings and college students—and those who will be there soon."

—JOE WHITE, president, Kanakuk

"I wish I'd had this book in my twenties! Get two copies, one for yourself and one for a friend! Grab a cup of coffee and discuss these gems of wisdom from young and old. You'll be amazed and refreshed!"

—SUSAN ALEXANDER YATES, speaker and best-selling author

PERSPECTIVES

PERSPECTIVES

A SPIRITUAL LIFE GUIDE FOR TWENTYSOMETHINGS

BY COLIN CREEL

[RELEVANTBOOKS]

Published by Relevant Books
A division of Relevant Media Group, Inc.

www.relevant-books.com
www.relevantmediagroup.com
© 2005 by Relevant Media Group, Inc.

Design by Relevant Solutions
Cover design Joshua Smith, Jeremy Kennedy, Aaron Maurer
Interior Design by Jeremy Kennedy, Aaron Maurer
www.relevant-solutions.com

For information or bulk orders:
RELEVANT MEDIA GROUP, INC.
100 SOUTH LAKE DESTINY DRIVE SUITE 200
ORLANDO, FL 32810
PH: (407) 660-1411

International Standard Book Number: 0976035782

05 06 07 08 09 8 7 6 5 4 3 2 1

Printed in the United States of America

To my parents
who have helped shape the right
perspective in me

PERSPECTIVES
CONTENTS

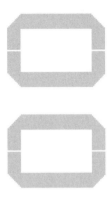

PREFACE

Journal Entry: 7/18/01, Age 26

As I watched *Dead Poets Society* for a few minutes
this evening, I wondered if I had/have ever truly lived.
What dreams have gotten lost along the journey from
adolescence until now? In less than two days, I will be
twenty-seven. By now, I would have assumed the thorn
in my flesh would have been removed; I'd be married
or seriously dating someone, and would have a clear picture of my vocational path. Fortunately or unfortunately,
depending on one's perspective, I've come to the realization the thorn will always tear at my flesh. Much like an
alcoholic, the successes lie in one's ability to manage the
affliction. I've learned so much about myself through

my struggles, while I often wonder where I would be today had I overcome my impediment at an early age. Am I the person I desired to be at twenty-seven? Much like Bruce Willis in *Unbreakable,* the only time he did not feel sadness in the morning was when he had saved people the night before. He served as he was created to do. Are my gifts truly to encourage and inspire? If so, what I am doing? When I wake up in the morning, do I feel true joy? Have I buried my childlike enthusiasm and youthful passion? Where has the fire escaped that once burned so ferociously? Father God, help me catch a clear vision for my life in line with Your will. May I be the man who longs to know You, to be with you and to worship You.

The twenties are formative years. Many decisions you make in your twenties affect the rest of your life for better or worse. Ironically, none of us are truly prepared or equipped to make those decisions. For the past nine years, I have sent weekly emails consisting mainly of book excerpts to encourage friends and family. As the years passed, I began to interweave my own thoughts. Over the past few years, peers have encouraged me to write a book. I always chuckled and thought, "What do I have to say? I am not an expert on anything." In March 2003, while listening to a sermon that wasn't particularly engaging for me, it hit me—write to encourage and inspire twentysomethings.

This project has many different angles: journals, writings, excerpts from Christian literature, pop culture examples, and life experiences. In addition, incorporated into each chapter is a section called "seasoned advice." The advice is derived from interviews in person or over email in which I've asked more seasoned individuals to reflect on their twenties with three simple questions:

(1) **What things do you wish you had known as a twentysomething?**

(2) **What were your biggest challenges in your twenties?**

(3) **What helped or hindered you from overcoming these challenges?**

People say the journey is more important than the destination. This journey has been long and hard, but well worth the effort to reach the final destination.

A special word of thanks to Tim Blue, a longtime friend who helped craft the vision and inspiration for this book. Thank you to Amy Hartman, Susan Yates, Lynn Barclay and my lovely fiancée, Krista, who have served as my champions throughout this long process; they never doubted this day would come to fruition. Professionally, Evan Hunter, Margaret Feinberg, Leslie Nunn Reed, Stan Carder, and Robert Wolgemuth all provided wonderful guidance along the way. In addition, thank you to my in-house editors: Kendra Morris, Amy Harper, and Charlie Woodward. Thank you also to the Wesleyan, Wake Forest and John Burroughs communities for their endless support and encouragement. Finally, I thank Him who began a good work in me. This book is truly His book about His people and for His people.

↗ ↙

HOW'S YOUR PERSPECTIVE?

"A mother enters her daughter's bedroom and sees a letter over the bed. With the worst premonition, she reads it, with trembling hands:

> It is with great regret and sorrow that I'm telling you that I eloped with my new boyfriend. I found real passion, and he is so nice, with all his piercings and tattoos and his big motorcycle. But it's not only that, Mom, I'm pregnant, and Ahmed said that we would be very happy in his trailer in the woods. He wants to have many more children with me, and that's one of my dreams. I've learned that marijuana doesn't hurt anyone, and we'll be growing it for us and his friends, who are providing us with all the cocaine and ecstasy we may want. In the

1

meantime, we'll pray for the science to find the AIDS cure, for Ahmed to get better, he deserves it. Don't worry Mom, I'm fifteen years old now, and I know how to take care of myself. Someday I'll visit for you to know your grandchildren. Your daughter, Judith

PS: Mom, it's not true. I'm at the neighbor's house. I just wanted to show you that there are worse things in life than the school's report card that's in my desk's drawer … I love you!" (anonymous email)

Perspective is a wonderful thing, isn't it? Within a ten-minute period I heard that a college friend's father unexpectedly passed away over the weekend followed by a student stopping by to inform me of his car accident in which no one was hurt, but he was obviously still upset about it. Life isn't always what you expect it to be.

As children we are always taught that we can do anything or be anyone. Life isn't always that easy though: accidents tragically take loved ones from us, hearts are broken; dreams die; thorns in our flesh repeatedly pierce us; doors close; we experience unfulfilling jobs; people long for a child or long for a spouse; and we wake up and ask, "Where has the time gone? Is this where I thought I would be? Is this how I thought my life would be?" Life isn't always what you expect it to be.

And yet, throughout Scripture it is clear that "in his heart a man plans his course, but the Lord determines his steps" (Prov. 16:9). In speaking with a dear friend this weekend, she reminded me that many of the great saints' lives in Scripture were drastically different than they thought they would be. As I drove home today, I scribbled down a few examples who come to mind, mainly, Moses, Paul, and Abraham.

Moses grew up as an Egyptian leading a pampered life in Pharaoh's palace. His world came crashing down when he witnessed an Egyptian guard beating a Hebrew slave. Sensing the injustice, Moses stepped in and ended up killing the guard. Realizing his act had become public knowledge, he fled. Soon after, he saved a flock of victimized women. A thankful father, Jethro, asked Moses to serve as a shepherd with him. Moses' second phase of life as a shepherd ran smoothly until God spoke to him and convinced the reluctant Moses to liberate His people. Not surprisingly, the Lord knew what He was doing. He knew the culmination of Moses' experiences would prepare him for his ultimate calling. Life isn't always what you expect it to be.

In the same way, Paul, a Roman and a Jew, was reared in a financially successful home, and by age thirteen, was an avid scholar who traveled to Jerusalem to study under the world-renowned Gamaliel. In Philippians, Paul states, "If anyone else thinks he has reasons to put confidence in the flesh, I have more: circumcised on the eighth day, of the people of Israel, of the tribe of Benjamin, a Hebrew of Hebrews; in regard to the law, a Pharisee; as for zeal, persecuting the church; as for legalistic righteousness, faultless" (Phil. 3:4-6). Paul was a young man who had the world by the tail, and yet the Lord had a different plan for him. He transformed Paul's passion, intellect, and zeal—once used to destroy the Church—to build the Church instead. Life isn't always what you expect it to be.

Unlike his colleagues, Abraham was Israel's founding father—a man of great faith who walked with God in obedience and enjoyed intimate fellowship with Him. At age seventy-five he was called to leave his "country, [his] people, and [his] father's household and go to the land I will show you" (Gen. 12:1). In addition, the Lord promised to make him into a great nation, bless him and his offspring, as well as give glory to his name. Years passed, and Abraham's wife remained barren. On numerous occasions, Abraham lied in order to make things go his way; he was far from perfect. And yet on the whole, Abraham remained faithful in the midst of extreme adversity. Then, when hope had run short, the Lord blessed him with a child whom He eventually asked Abraham to sacrifice. Life isn't always what you expect it to be.

3

All of these men had to withstand extreme adversity, times of uncertainty, and times of waiting. These challenges all served their purpose: to prepare these men so that they might give God the most glory by their lives. J.I. Packer suggests in *Knowing God* that: "These things are written for our learning, for the same wisdom that ordered the paths which God's saints trod in Bible times orders the Christian's life today. We should not, therefore, be too taken aback when unexpected and upsetting and discouraging things happen to us now. What do they mean? Simply that God in His wisdom means to make something of us which we have not attained yet, and He is dealing with us accordingly." Ultimately, our heart's desire should be to give God the most glory. God has wonderful things in store for our lives if we can stay the course, remain obedient, and never give up hope in His promises. In those challenging times when our lives aren't what we expect them to be, do you find yourself asking, "Where's God?"

Here's an illustration that might help refocus your gaze: Where's Waldo? Where's Waldo? Yes, that red-and-white striped-shirt-and-glasses-wearing young lad who enjoys hiding himself in pictures. You know he's in the picture, but sometimes he is easier to find than others. The more time spent staring at Where's Waldo pictures, the easier it is to find Him because you know what he looks like. In the same way, the clearer the picture you have of Christ, the easier it will be to find him in the midst of all the confusion. Fixate your eyes on Christ, and everything else will fall by the wayside. Let the saints' lives of the past serve as hope for your future. Life isn't always what you expect it to be, but stay obedient, cling to His promises, and it can be even better: "Trust in the Lord with all your heart and lean not on your own understanding; in all your ways acknowledge him, and he will make your paths straight" (Prov. 3:5-6).

Seasoned Advice

Nancy Beach, 47, teaching pastor/programming director at Willow Creek Community Church, Barrington, Illinois: In my twenties, I learned that I could experience the loss of a dream and trust God to redirect me toward another fulfilling passion.

After college, my dream was to become a producer/director of high impact, excellent films and/or television programs. I sincerely believed my pursuit of that dream would most honor God with the gifts entrusted to me. My plan was to marry late (if at all) and move to Los Angeles. But then I met Warren, and in just ten months we chose to get married. That proved to be a great decision by far, but Warren's business was squarely planted in the Chicago area. So was a church I helped launch called Willow Creek. Our church had a very bumpy first few years, caused by the sins and immaturity of all of us young leaders. I was hurt in the early years of the church, and very tentative about continuing ministry there. But my heavenly Father guided me to invest my artistic gifts and dreams in the local church, specifically at Willow. I thought at first that was a loser option. Twenty-one years later, I am deeply grateful for a ministry adventure I never could have imagined. God replaced my original dream with one that fits me, stretches me, and fulfills me to my toes. I could never have predicted this in my twenties. I had no idea. And now when life doesn't go according to my plans, I try to remember that God just might have a better idea …

Points to Ponder

1. How is your life different than you expected it to be?

2. What adversity has been the most difficult to overcome?

3. What have you learned through that adversity?

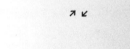

WHAT MAKES YOU POUND THE TABLE?

"What makes you pound on the table?" —Howard Hendricks

↗ ↙ ↗ ↙ ↗

Howard Hendricks is one of my friend's heroes. Though he's fast approaching his eightieth birthday, apparently he is a man still full of enthusiasm and vigor. Believing in people who don't believe in themselves is his main gift, one that has changed countless lives directly and even more indirectly through those he's encouraged. As a senior in college, my friend Tim spent the entire first semester considering what career he might choose. Business was his major, but little interested him in the world of business. Teaching appealed to him, but he knew little about the profession, so he called Dr. Hendricks to ask what it takes to be a

7

teacher. During his ten-minute conversation Dr. Hendricks gave plenty of great advice, but he asked one question that still stands out for Tim: "Tim," he said, "what makes you pound on the table?" He wanted to know what Tim lost sleep thinking about,

what raised his blood pressure, what stirred his soul. For Tim, the answer was and still is teaching. He absolutely loves to teach; he loves to give people an "aha" experience, to take them from a dark place of confusion to the light place of comprehension. Regardless of the subject matter or content, Tim has an incredible way of distilling difficult concepts into easily digestible morsels. He loves to teach.

I, on the other hand, still have difficulty pinpointing my singular passion. I do not know what makes me pound on the table. I know many things drive me to tap on the table though. I imagine I am more the norm than Tim. Throughout our lives many of us have been told we can do anything on which we set our minds. How many of us have been told we could be doctors, lawyers, or astronauts? Sky's the limit. I have been blessed with a mother who is a relentless encourager. As a result, I believe I can accomplish nearly anything upon which I set my mind. What a wonderful blessing to have been given; however, pouring my energies into one activity proves a daunting challenge for me. I desire excellence in a bevy of areas but lack the time to achieve all of them. Over the years, I have learned more about what I do not enjoy doing more than what tasks I do enjoy. Obviously, my means will take longer than Tim's, but thankfully, I have begun to accept that for one reason or another the Lord has chosen to keep His overarching plan hidden from me. My theme verse is: "From everyone who has been given much, much will be demanded; and from the one who has been entrusted with much, much more will be asked" (Luke 12:48b). The Lord places miniature visions on my heart to keep me motivated; He knows exactly what I need in order to stay driven. The twenties is a time of discovery of who you are, but more importantly whose you are. Take time to reflect on the way in which God has wired you.

Since leaving college years ago, I have seen people do all sorts of jobs: banking, medicine, law, sales, and so on, but I've seen very few people with any real passion or vision. Most of them take jobs either for money or because it's what looks good in the eyes of society. The ones who are passionate aren't hard to spot. There's Kit, who talks about science and medicine in a way that restores my faith in the world of medicine; there's Matt, who had a vision to start a church in St. Louis geared toward young adults; and there's Brad, who loves the teenagers he teaches with more compassion than they may ever again see. There are some others, too, but they are exceptions to the rule. Most people are bored and even miserable in their work. For them it's all about a paycheck and putting food on the table. Work is only a means to an end, not something worthwhile for its own sake. They don't pound the table over anything, except maybe their frustration with a boring life. It is often said Americans live to work while Europeans work to live. Where do you fall? The following story I received over email, author unknown, illustrates our misdirection with vocation:

> The American investment banker was at the pier of a small coastal Mexican village when a small boat with just one fisherman docked. Inside the small boat were several large yellow-fin tuna. The American complimented the Mexican on the quality of his fish and asked how long it took to catch them.
>
> The Mexican replied, only a little while.
>
> The American then asked why didn't he stay out longer and catch more fish?
>
> The Mexican said he had enough to support his family's immediate needs.
>
> The American then asked, "But what do you do with the rest of your time?"
>
> The Mexican fisherman said, "I sleep late, fish a little, play with my children, take siesta with my wife, Maria, stroll into the village each evening where I sip wine and play guitar with my amigos. I have a full and busy life."

The American scoffed, "I am a Harvard MBA and could help you. You should spend more time fishing and with the proceeds, buy a bigger boat. With the proceeds from the bigger boat, you could buy several boats. Eventually you would have a fleet of fishing boats. Instead of selling your catch to a middleman, you would sell directly to the processor, eventually opening your own cannery. You would control the product, processing, and distribution. You would need to leave this small coastal fishing village and move to Mexico City, then LA and eventually NYC where you would run your expanding enterprise."

The Mexican fisherman asked, "But, how long will this all take?"

To which the American replied, "Fifteen to twenty years."

"But what then?"

The American laughed and said that's the best part. "When the time is right, you would announce an IPO and sell your company stock to the public and become very rich. You would make millions."

"Millions ... Then what?"

The American said, "Then you would retire. Move to a small coastal fishing village where you would sleep late, fish a little, play with your kids, take siesta with your wife, stroll to the village in the evenings where you could sip wine and play your guitar with your amigos."

As a young person you still have the choice to make. Perhaps you love acting, animals, or building things. Like it or not, work will consume the majority of your adult life. When you go to a party, the first question out of everyone's mouth to a stranger is, "What do you do?" We identify people by their jobs, and perhaps this is why so many of us do unfulfilling jobs: We want to impress strangers at cocktail parties. After all, "I'm a CEO" sounds more prestigious than "I'm a struggling actor." But who wants to be a CEO if it means giving up your passion? Trust me, no amount of money can make up for a lack of fulfillment with your job. If you don't trust me, ask a rich person if his money makes him happy. Ask him if he's doing what he really loves. As you face the question of what to do with your career, you'll have to come to terms with things like how much money you want to make (or can live on), what lifestyle you want in terms of free time, what other people will think of you, etc. These are difficult questions, some of which I'm still dealing with and expect to for a while. But I guarantee you this: If it's something that makes you pound on the table, you are likely to find it satisfying. Don't settle for mediocrity! Esau (Gen. 25:29-34) sold God's best, in this case his birthright, for red stew. It seems ridiculous, but how often do we settle for instantaneous gratification in lieu of God's jewels that shine against the backdrop of eternity? Be willing to forge ahead with a career in which you find it surprising to get paid for having such fun. You'll never regret it, no matter how small the paycheck may be. What stirs your soul? When do tears well up in your eyes? What makes you pound the table?

↗ ↙ ↗ ↙ ↗

Seasoned Advice

Jim Pope, 47, president of Pope Automotive Groups in Atlanta, Georgia: As I reflect back on my twenties, I am sorely reminded of what a different time it was. My biggest concern was getting out of college as quickly as possible so that I could get on with my career in the automobile business, get out on my own, and start a family. I was married at twenty-two; we had our first child at twenty-six, and started our own dealership at twenty-eight. I had life figured out. What I wish I had known was that life did not have to be rushed. At twenty, young men and women should experience life, try different things, study different subjects, travel, make mistakes, have fun. There is plenty of time to work, and if not, then I believe God would have wanted us to experience this life to the fullest.

What I didn't know then was that circumstances and blessings from God dictated great success, not my abilities. The late eighties brought economic challenges that led all the way into the early nineties, and they were humbling indeed. Nothing came easy, and long, hard hours to stay afloat brought family stresses and neglected relationships. What I learned was success lies in building lasting relationships—relationships with family, friends, and certainly God—not in how many cars or widgets you can sell. Regarding careers, what I know now is the highs can never be too high, because the lows are never as low as they seem. God calls us to never be too taken with ourselves and also to never judge ourselves too harshly. But it is the relationships with the people that experience both of those with you, the highs and the lows, which will make the difference in your life and will be your most proud accomplishments.

Bryan Coley, 38, artistic director of Art Within, Atlanta, Georgia: My twenties were a time of compliance. I felt that life was pretty much a path or rather a checklist of accomplishments, which I had to begin checking off. There was college, getting a job, advancing in that job, finding a wife, marrying that wife, and getting a house. All of which I think I pretty much achieved in my twenties. By my thirties, someone finally asked me the question: "If you won the lottery, what would you do?" Having to answer that question forced me to revisit what I was doing. I answered, "I'd open up a theater company." My friend asked me, "Why wasn't I doing it now?" It was the best question anyone ever asked me. It brought me to my passion … what I was created to be and do versus what I was doing out of what I thought I should do or what I thought my parents thought I should do. My twenties were not wasted. I went to NYU film school. I worked at Turner Broadcasting. I dated and married my beautiful wife. However, I look back at my twenties as just preparation for my thirties, a time spent learning, growing into an understanding of what I wanted. I don't think you can get around this learning period, when you are understanding your newfound freedom and trying to free yourself from your parents' expectations. However, I look back at my time at NYU and think, "Man, I wish I could have had the passion I have now and the confidence and security of my talents and gifting during my time at NYU."

Points to Ponder

1. What do you dream of as the perfect life?

2. What would you do if you could make $1 million doing anything?

3. What is most frightening to you as you consider pursuing your dream?

4. What is the greatest risk of pursuing your dream? Is it worth it?

5. What is the greatest risk of not pursuing your dream? Is it worth it?

6. Read Matthew 6:19-24. Where is your treasure?

WHY IS IT IMPORTANT FOR ME TO HAVE A PAUL, A BARNABAS, AND A TIMOTHY?

I've never run a full marathon before, but I've run enough races to understand the role other runners play in spurring one another on toward a maximized team performance. In every race, much like in life, runners often encounter three types of people: those who pull you along, those you run alongside, and those you pull along. Scripture offers excellent illustrations of this principle.

As the writer of thirteen of the twenty-seven books in the New Testament, Paul's wisdom, insight, and experience were critical in the growth of the early church. In Philippians he states, "If anyone else thinks he has reasons to put confidence in the flesh, I have more: circumcised on the eighth day, of the people of Israel, of the tribe of Benjamin, a Hebrew of Hebrews; in regard to the law, a Pharisee; as for zeal, persecuting the church; as for legalistic righteousness, faultless" (Phil. 3:4-6). He goes on to call all of his worldly accolades "rubbish" in comparison to the joy of knowing Christ. Paul spent the better part of his life starting churches and then continuing to encourage those churches through letters. He also sent letters to those whom he mentored, most notably, Timothy.

Despite his usefulness on earth, Paul still longed to go home. He longed to be with his Creator. However, He knew his role in the kingdom. He understood his life served as the benchmark for many of his contemporaries. He longed to go home, but cast aside his personal desires for the benefit of others:

> For to me, to live is Christ and to die is gain. If I am to go on living in this body, this will mean fruitful labor for me. Yet what shall I choose? I do not know! I am torn between the two: I desire to depart and be with Christ, which is better by far; but it is more necessary for you that I remain in the body. Convinced of this, I know that I will remain, and I will continue with all of you for your progress and joy in the faith, so that through my being with you again your joy in Christ Jesus will overflow on account of me. (Phil 1:21-26)

Timothy was one of those individuals whom Paul pulled up during his journey: "Paul wanted to take him along the journey, so he circumcised him because of the Jews who lived in that area, for they all knew that his father was a Greek" (Acts 16:3). Paul served as a father figure for Timothy by challenging, supporting, and providing him opportunities for growth. Paul's affection for Timothy is evident as he calls him, "Timothy my true son in the faith" (1 Tim. 1:2). Much like a father, Paul trained Timothy according to God's Word for a season, then sent him out to prove himself in Corinth: "For this reason I am sending to you Timothy, my son whom I love, who is faithful in the Lord. He will remind you of my way of life in Christ Jesus, which agrees with what I teach everywhere in every church" (1 Cor. 4:17). I am struck by the phrase, "he will remind you of my way of life in Christ Jesus." Isn't that often the case when you emulate someone? Often your mannerisms, your vernacular, and your appearance resemble that person or group of people whom you emulate. This principle reinforces the importance of choosing one's Paul appropriately.

Paul's prominence in the early church came quickly, but "when he came to Jerusalem, he tried to join the disciples, but they were all afraid of him, not believing that he was really a disciple. But Barnabas took him and brought him to the apostles. He told them how Saul on his journey had seen the Lord and that the Lord had spoken to him, and how in Damascus he had preached fearlessly in the name of Jesus" (Acts 9:26-27). The disciples did not trust Saul, but they trusted their friend Barnabas. Barnabas ran alongside Paul; he believed in Paul and thus opened the door with the disciples. Not surprisingly, the name Barnabas literally means "son of encouragement." Luke describes Barnabas as "a good man, full of the Holy Spirit and faith, and a great number of people were brought to the Lord" (Acts 11:24). Barnabas assisted Paul on many missionary journeys. Throughout Acts, Barnabas and Paul are synonymous; for instance, "then Barnabas went to Tarsus to look for Saul, and when he found him, he brought him to Antioch. So for a whole year Barnabas and Saul met with the church and taught great numbers of people. The disciples were called Christians first at Antioch" (Acts 11:25-26). Entrenched in ministry, these two men encouraged and motivated one another.

Identifying individuals who fill these roles in your life is imperative to your spiritual development. Since leaving Winston-Salem, two of these roles have been more challenging for me, and I have felt the void in my life. Recently, I have recommitted to filling these voids.

↗ ↙ ↗ ↙ ↗

Seasoned Advice

Dr. Charles H. Talbert, 70, distinguished professor of religion, Baylor University, Texas: Mentors have been crucial for me, especially in my twenties. When I started to college, my father and I drove to campus. On the way he said, "Son, you never have to be afraid of your mind. If you pursue truth far enough with your mind, you will come out OK." Hence, I started to college without a fear of my mind. In college I had a religion professor who embodied the same lesson. He listened patiently to my questions and theories. When he did not know an answer, he said so. He also said that I should continue to pursue, without fear, answers that he did not have. He indicated that I should not be afraid of religious experience, just as I should not be afraid of my mind. In seminary I again had a professor with the same attitude. He would stay after class to listen and to advise. He was so well educated that he saw the big picture. He would say, "Yes, you are right, but that is only a part of the answer. Go explore." He said this about my religious experience as well as my intellectual quest. In graduate school I once again had such a professor. He would say to my expressions of frustration, "Yes, those concerns are real. We all have been through them. Stay the course. You will find your way through the tangle." All of these mentors, who I knew prior to turning thirty, contributed to my striving for a synthesis of faith and reason.

Points to Ponder

1. Who challenges you?
   Who gives you opportunities for growth?
   Who's your Paul?

2. Who stands beside you?
   Who encourages you unconditionally?
   Who's your Barnabas?

3. Who do you challenge?
   To whom do you impart your wisdom?
   Who's your Timothy?

WHAT ARE YOUR STANDARDS?

I'd like to share a story I heard from Tommy Nelson a few years ago that always weighs heavily on my heart. Once upon a time there was a community of people who lived near a river. One day a man came to visit this community. This community of people was extremely hospitable and opened up its village to the visitor. While they were enjoying a meal together near the river, all of a sudden a crocodile leapt out of the river and chomped a man's arm off. Everyone was horrified; villagers quickly assisted the man and took him away. Once the body was removed from the table, the host resumed eating as if nothing had transpired. The visitor looked around in amazement and said, "Did you not just see what happened?" The host replied, "We did; it is unfortunate, but in our culture it is inappropriate to talk about crocodiles." As the man took a closer look at the community, he noticed there

19

were dozens of people with portions of their bodies missing. Some were missing arms, legs, pieces of back, and yet no one did anything to protect themselves from crocodiles. No one hunted them down. No one found out where they lay their heads because it was inappropriate in their culture to talk about crocodiles.

SEX. In our culture it is inappropriate to talk about sex, and yet the media bombards us with sex everywhere we turn—in the grocery line, on the Internet, and on television. Our generation has instantaneous access to anything we desire. And yet, too often we do not discuss sex in its proper context. I'm still waiting for my parents to talk to me about sex. The night before I started my first day of college, my dad sat me down and started to have "the talk." I quickly assured him we didn't need to have the "the talk," much to his relief. I added that I already had learned everything from the walls of the corner gas station. How many of us have chunks missing out of bodies because of sex? How many of us have placed our needs and desires before God's? How many of us have been disobedient in the area of sexual purity?

Having worked with college and high school students during the last nine years, it is painfully apparent that most people, even Christians, have preferences, but lack convictions. You may not be having sex, but is it because of your devotion to God or fear of what your peers may think? Would it matter if your peers felt differently? Guard yourself threefold: guard your mind, guard your heart, and guard your body.

Guard your mind: Summer of 2002 I attended teacher camp. I was surrounded by some of the best and brightest young teachers in the nation. I quickly learned when you place a group of twenty- and thirty-year-olds in a dorm for a few weeks, everyone's maturation process regresses. Staying up late, cliques, partying all night, practical jokes, and profanity abounded. It amazed me how many people were dropping the "f-bomb" so effortlessly. By the end of the last week, although none ever slipped out, in my mind I was cussing like a sailor without even knowing it. The old saying is true—garbage in, garbage out. In the exact same way, visual images have an even greater effect on your ideology or the way in which you view life. Images can potentially control your mind: "You have heard that it was said, 'Do not commit adultery.' But I tell you that anyone who looks at a woman lustfully has already committed adultery with her in his heart" (Matt. 5:27-28). The first time I ever heard this verse was the summer after my freshman year in high school. I attended a Christian family camp, Northern Pines, with another family because I had a crush on this girl who was going. During that week, for the first time, I learned that sex before marriage was wrong. In addition, the leader described that even thinking about sex was wrong. OK, so I'm a fourteen-year-old-boy: I'm just starting to grow, my voice is deepening to a manly voice, and my hormones are raging ... and now I learn that even thinking about sex is wrong. That was it; I was going to hell. Lightning was about to strike me down because all I was thinking about was sex and sports; sex and sports; sports and sex.

Actions begin in your mind. What are your standards? Do you make allowances for the flesh? Do you make separate housing accommodations on trips? Do you dim lights, insert mood music, and hope for the best? God demands purity, not only outward purity, but inward purity ... of thoughts. What are you watching? What are you reading? "Do not arouse or awaken love until it so desires" (Song of Sol. 2:7). Guard your mind.

Guard your heart: Sexual purity is an issue of lordship. Who is in control, you or God? My old pastor used to always say, "Lord of all or not at all." When you start to fool around sexually, as Tommy Nelson says, it is as if you are placing your tongue on a flagpole in Alaska. That is an ill-designed union; you are not going to leave that relationship without leaving a portion of yourself on that pole. Sex is wonderful ... or at least that's what my friends tell me. God created it, but it is meant for two individuals whose hearts are forever linked in marriage. Often, we get caught in the trap of comparing our sexual indulgences with others. My social apex occurred in junior high. I stood all of four-foot eleven with blonde hair, and performed in the school musicals. I thought I was the stuff. I remember switching dates four or five times for the Sadie Hawkins Dance in seventh grade. I dated a different girl every week, including one of Trista's (the Bachelorette) best friends. Needless to say, I was a jerk. No one knew why I dumped all of those girls though. If the truth be told, I was afraid of kissing them. I later learned many of my friends experimented sexually because they thought I was more advanced than I was. God is your standard, not your peer group.

Sexually charged relationships will continue to diminish over time. It will take more and more in order to reach that jolt. How far is too far? As you have probably heard before, you are asking the wrong question ... how pure is too pure? I am a twenty-nine-year-old virgin by God's grace. I do not desire for my wedding night to be business as usual. We are all blameful in the area of sexual impurity. Thankfully, in Scripture it says that God can restore what the locusts have eaten, "therefore if anyone is in Christ, he is a new creation; the old is gone, the new has come!" (2 Cor. 5:17). One of my favorite verses is, "Blessed are the pure in heart for they shall see God" (Matt. 5:8). Do you see God when the lights are off? Do you see God when you are alone in your apartment with candles lit and mood music? "Do not arouse or awaken love until it so desires" (Song of Sol. 2:7). Guard your heart.

Guard your body: "Flee from sexual immorality. All other sins a man commits are outside his body, but he who sins sexually, sins against his own body. Do you not know that your body is a temple of the Holy Spirit, who is in you, whom you have received from God? You are not your own, you were bought at a price. Therefore honor God with your body" (1 Cor. 6:18-20). One of the best ways to honor God with your body is to help out your brother and sister in Christ. Guys, women are aroused by touch, so be careful about showing affection prematurely. Ladies, guys are aroused by sight; modest in apparel is a must.

God declares in 1 Thessalonians 4, "Each of you should learn to control his own body in a way that is holy and honorable, not a passionate lust like the heathens who do not know God ... for

God did not call us to be impure, but to live a holy life. There-fore, he who rejects this instruction does not reject man but God, who gives his Holy Spirit." Setting up rules for myself has always helped me. Know your limits. My college roommate and I kept each other accountable our senior year. We were both dating girls who lived in the same suite. We had to be home by 12:30 a.m. Nothing good ever happens after midnight. I imagine there is some scientific study about this, but it seems like when you get tired, your inhibitions are lowered and you do not always make the wisest decisions. My roommate married his girlfriend, and my girlfriend and I broke up. She said, "Thank you for keeping me pure." She's now married. We loved each other and wanted to be with each other, but we both had convictions. We were not going to tarnish our relationship with Christ for one another, even if it meant losing each other. "Do not arouse or awaken love until it so desires" (Song of Sol. 2:7). Guard your body.

↗ ↙ ↗ ↙ ↗

Seasoned Advice

Bryan Coley, 38, artistic director of Art Within, Atlanta, Georgia: As for regrets or struggles, I think the biggest struggle of my twenties was premarital sex. I almost married the wrong girl because of it, and my wife and I struggle with intimacy today because of our inability to control our lust for each other before marriage. As a Christian, my wife and I cannot look back to our dating period in our twenties with great nostalgia because when-ever we point to a certain special moment, it was tainted with sex. This is such a huge issue right now in a culture that says the opposite, but trust me, you have to view your twenties as a time of patiently waiting, with self-control for God's future. I think if most married people were honest about who had premarital sex, they would tell you (or maybe they wouldn't even know) that the lack of a really great sex life in marriage or the inability to really connect our sexual experience in marriage with true intimacy is because of using up "the magic dust" of this blending of intimacy

23

and sex before marriage. And, as a Christian, you look back with regret instead of the joy that should be accompanied with getting to open up and use the magic dust.

Points to Ponder

1. Actions begin in your mind.
   What are your standards?

2. "Blessed are the pure in heart for they shall see God" (Matt. 5:8).
   What obstacles are keeping you from seeing God?

3. Your body is the temple of God, bought at a price.
   It is not your own. Are you defiling God by your treatment of your body or someone else's?

WHERE DO YOU FIND YOUR IDENTITY?

Journal Entry: 8/13/01, Age 27

The last few days have been difficult. Clothed in self-pity I mask from others the erosion occurring inside me. I feel like a shell of the man I once was. Priorities out of whack, lack of discipline, and lack of vision catapult me into a downward spiral. Struggling to climb out by my own will, I realize over and over Christ beckons, "Abide in Me." The line between trust and fear is miniscule, but Christ calls us to trust in Him. I'm always trying to "fix" things. Rest in me. Take things slowly. Am I truly serving God? My wheels are spinning, but am I going in the right direction or even behind the wheel of the wrong automobile? I desperately desire to be in Your will, but

25

have I stifled the still, small voice which once wouldn't allow me to walk by a piece of trash without picking it up? Is my lifestyle unaccommodating to listening? Unbind me from these shackles and set me free from myself. I want every aspect of my life to be a living testimony to You. Forgive me when I don't make/take time for others. Selfless is not a quality I would ever use to describe myself. Ambition, peer's approval, and ego block my road to a saintly life. I want this year to be different. Help me and show me necessary changes to live unabashedly for You, Father. Let Your light shine through me. Let Your will be my will; let selflessness radiate from my exterior; cleanse my motives and wash my soul. May You be proud of my thoughts, my deeds, and my life."

In your twenties, it is surprisingly difficult not to associate your worth with work. We are a performance-driven society. What am I producing? How are my services beneficial? What can I offer that others might want? My time? My abilities? My passion? My vision? As a borderline type A, slightly OCD personality, producing results is a big part of how God wired me. That is not necessarily bad. The world needs movers and shakers, but one's greatest strength is more often than not one's greatest challenge. Human nature will pull people to where they receive strokes for their accomplishments. I often wonder if people really enjoy doing certain things, or if it is merely because they receive accolades for a particular talent or skill. I imagine it is probably a little bit of both. Strokes are addictive, and much like sex, they fall under the law of diminishing returns. You will continually have to produce more to receive the same jolt of encouragement. This cycle will repeat itself unless your motivation, your content- ment, and your identity reside in Christ.

Am I Enough?

Does your devotion to me depend
on my willingness to bless you?
Am I Enough?
"Consider it pure joy, my brothers, whenever you face trials of
many kinds, because you know that the testing of your faith
develops perseverance" (James 1:2-3).
Am I Enough?
Where did I say happiness is more important than character?
Am I Enough?
"Wait for the Lord, be strong and
take heart and wait for the Lord" (Ps. 27:14).
Am I Enough?
Where does your trust reside?
Am I Enough?
"In his heart a man plans his course,
but the Lord determines his steps" (Prov. 16:9).
Am I Enough?
Upon what is your joy dependent?
Am I Enough?
"Have I not commanded you? Be strong and courageous. Do not
be terrified; do not be discouraged, for the Lord your God will
be with you wherever you go" (Josh. 1:9).
Am I Enough?
"…do you truly love Me more than these?"
"Feed my lambs."
"…do you truly love me?"
"Take care of my sheep."
"Do you love me?"
Jesus said, "Feed my sheep" (John 21).
Am I Enough?

The Lord is so good to us. As I reread this poem I wrote many
months ago, tears fill my eyes. Do I truly believe God is enough?
Or is it God plus a respectable career? Or is it God plus others

thinking highly of me? Or is it God plus a wonderful marriage and family? Or is it God plus a long happy, healthy life? Who am I to make provisions on God?

↗ ↙ ↗ ↙ ↗

Seasoned Advice

Lynn Barclay, 44, regional director of Young Life, Winston-Salem, North Carolina: I believe the biggest need of twentysomethings is for spiritual direction that will help them to discern between what they "feel" and what is the call of God on their life. Sometimes that is one and the same, but more times than not it is two different things. The need to take "all thoughts captive to the obedience of Christ" is more pressing than ever in a culture that is inundated with information from every arena.

Jim Reed, 46, Worship Leader at First Presbyterian Church, Winston-Salem, North Carolina: Email August 14, 2001: Colin, you can't do enough. You'll never be able to do enough, be enough, have enough, serve enough, give enough, pray enough, worship enough, study enough, or submit yourself enough to whatever rigors you think might smooth some of the rough edges and bring you closer to God. He, on the other hand, has done everything so that you can be His, be faithful, be attentive, and be walking in the immense freedom of His grace to discover more of Him, His love, His work in you, His will for your life, His best use for your gifts, His direction for your life. Be present to the Lord now, for what He has put before you right now; be present to the students you have been given to love and mentor; present to the other faculty who need loving leadership and shepherding; present to the people in your life who love you for where you are right now. Take your eyes off the horizon and what might be, or could be. Focus on what the Lord has put before you right now, be faithful to fulfill His call for you right now. When it's time to look up on the horizon to see what the Lord is bringing your way, He will tell you to look up and get ready for what lies ahead. Until then, be faithful and purposeful to find your significance in doing your best to fulfill God's call on your life right now. The accolades may or may not come, but that will not matter if you know at the core of who you are that you are fulfilling God's call on your life. What would matter would be that you strove for the accolades and public recognition of your accomplishments and in the process sacrificed being in the center of God's will for your life. You will have achieved something good at the possible cost of God's best for you.

I love you.

Jim

Points to Ponder

1. Is God enough for you?

2. What provisions do you add to the statement, "God is enough plus ..."?

3. What can you do to remove the shackles from your perception of God?

WHAT CLAMORS
FOR YOUR
ATTENTION?

We're all born with one thing in common: time. Not everyone is born with money or good parents or good genetic makeup, but we are all born with some amount of time to spend. The average person gets around seventy years. Some get far fewer, some get far more. But regardless of how much you get, you have a responsibility to spend it well. Imagine spending one dollar every second. Some you spend on candy, some on entertainment, some on giving to the needy and so on. Time is no different. As each moment passes, you have spent a moment that can never return. You may have invested it in time with a friend or you may have wasted it watching commercials, but you can't get it back. How we spend our time plays out in a series of choices, every moment, every day.

31

The Christian life would be far easier if God was a little more direct and demanding. Dogs demand to be fed; kids demand to be played with; bosses demand that you show up for work; but the demands God places on our time are subtle and altogether inaudible. Falling victim to the tyranny of that which is loud, demanding, and urgent, most of us crawl in bed each night exhausted, wondering where the day went, wondering when the peace and quiet we long for will finally rescue us from all the noise. In other words, Charles Swindoll says: "Guard against the tyranny of the urgent. The most important things will seldom scream for your attention, they will simply wait for you to discover them. Things like prayer, Scripture study, cultivating friendships, thinking, enjoying art. The loud and demanding are rarely as important as these."[1]

In his book, *Intimacy with the Almighty*, Charles Swindoll also paints a picture of two sailboats at sea traveling in opposite directions. Both ships use the same wind, blowing from the same direction, yet one takes the easy path allowing the wind to carry it along with its (the wind's) direction, while the other boat travels against the wind.[2] The wind represents all that demands our attention in life: TV, phone calls, fast food, entertainment, shopping … but there is a choice to be made whether to be swept along with the current of society, allowing others to dictate how we should spend our time or to go against the flow by making our own choices. Clearly, the latter choice is more difficult, but it has the long-term effect of getting you to your goal.

Time with God can be difficult. Rarely is it as entertaining as a *Seinfeld* or *Friends* rerun or as immediately gratifying as another thirty minutes of sleep. Most days, in fact, discouragement seems to sit next to me as I try to read my Bible or to pray. It whispers in my ear, bringing questions to my mind: Is this really worth the time? What am I supposed to get out of this? Why can't I have life-changing revelations every time I open the Bible? Will my prayers ever get answered the way I want? Much like training for an athletic event, the discipline of time with God is hard to maintain without an understanding of one's goal(s). Imagine shooting one hundred free throws every day but never playing on a basketball team, never getting the chance to make the winning basket as the clock runs out, never reaching a goal. In my estimation, personal devotions are so easy to overlook because we have few, if any, clear objectives in mind about the purpose of that time. Out of obligation or legalism, we read our chapter a day, say our prayers for close friends and family, and check it off our to do list with a sigh of relief, looking forward to Sunday when we don't feel quite so obligated to spend time alone with God. Or pressed with yet another busy day, we make a guilt-ridden promise to God to get up earlier tomorrow, knowing full well that tomorrow's calendar is even fuller. Perhaps we never even think of it at all but still have a looming suspicion that having a personal relationship with God really ought to involve actual communication every now and then.

If your goal is to experience the joys and successes of the world, the answer is to simply get up each morning and allow the people, TV shows and billboards around you to tell you how to get where you're going. We carve out time for these items in our lives that we deem important. How many times have you rearranged your schedule to watch an athletic competition, spend time with friends, or hear the latest band? There is no lack of worldly resources for getting rich quickly, meeting a beautiful woman, or owning the home of your dreams before you can afford it, but these treasures will not last. They are easy, short sighted goals: "Yet when I surveyed all that my hands had done and what I had toiled to achieve, everything was meaningless, a chasing after the wind; nothing was gained under the sun" (Eccles. 2:11). On the other hand, if you desire eternal rewards and riches, you must swim upstream, and for that you will need God's help. Keeping this in mind, our time with God takes on a whole new meaning: Difficult days are welcomed as a training ground, just as a challenging workout yields the most results. "Good" days are greeted with joy and thankfulness, like finding a workout easy when a hard one was expected. Neither type of time with God will ever stop coming. During some periods you'll have lots of difficult days or lots of easy, peaceful days, but no mountaintop experience lasts nor does any valley experience. If our goal is to accomplish God's purposes, we must learn the discipline of faith that will see us through the hard times and give us great joy in the easy times.

↗ ↙ ↗ ↙ ↗

Seasoned Advice

Mike Duke, 54, president and CEO of Wal-Mart Stores, Rogers, Arkansas: As a twentysomething, many activities outside of my marriage vied for my attention, most notably my education, my career, as well as my stint with the National Guard. As a result, I spent less time with my children in their early years than I would have hoped. It wasn't until my early forties that I truly understood the importance of expressing affection toward children in their early years while serving as a foster parent for an adorable child, Jennifer, from three months to nineteen months.

A child's proper development hinges on a multitude of affection. Hold your child. Verbally affirm your child. I was a different parent in my forties, and I am forever grateful to have those months with Jennifer. Every time I visit with Jennifer, she serves as a reminder of a very important lesson in my life.

Bill Haslam, 46, Mayor of Knoxville, Tennessee, and former President of Saks Direct and Pilot Corporation: When I look back on my twenties, I am reminded of a time in my life that was rich with change, opportunity, and activity. However, it also makes me think about a time when I was incredibly unfocused and clueless about how to use my time and gifts effectively. My wife and I were married a year after college and had three kids by the time we were thirty. I had a job that required me to work a lot of hours and to be out of town a couple of nights a week. In addition to marriage, a busy job, and little kids, we were teaching the college Sunday school class, volunteering for Young Life, and beginning to be involved in children's activities.

I think it was at that point in time that I began to pick up the bad side-effects of multitasking. Now, believe me, there is nothing wrong with multitasking on some things. I like to watch the news when I am getting dressed in the morning. I have even learned how to answer emails and listen to voicemails at the same time. The bad side-effect that I developed was the habit of never being completely engaged in whatever I was doing. The Jim Elliot quote, "Wherever you are, be all there," comes to mind. When it came time to listen to a sermon, I needed to be listening to a sermon. When it was time to address an issue with a work colleague, he or she should get my full attention—not the remnants of my brain while I thought about the next issue of the day. Most importantly, my wife deserved all of me! For some strange reason, she didn't regard it as being "more efficient" when I was doing something else while listening to her.

In hindsight, my twenties was the time when life's possibilities collided with the reality that having a job and a family was much more time-consuming than the requirements of being in college. I wish I had done a better job early on of sorting out those things that I was called to do from those things that were screaming loudly for my attention.

Points to Ponder

1. Do others dictate your time?

2. What measures do you have in place to help guard against the current of society?

3. What are the most important areas in your life? Does your time reflect that devotion?

1. From a letter to author's friend, Tim Blue.
2. Charles Swindoll, *Intimacy with the Almighty* (Word Publishing, Dallas, TX: 1996) p. 34.

HOW DO
YOU HANDLE
ADVERSITY?

During the fall of 2004 I traveled to take part in a wedding. I met the couple when I was working at a college and leading Quest, a Young Life leadership training program. Paul was in my small group, and Erin was the focus of many freshmen admirers. Even as freshmen, these two had hearts for Christ coupled with wonderful relational and discernment gifts. When Paul and Erin asked me to sing in their wedding, I was truly honored.

The honor grew even more when I heard the tragic news that Paul's father had a heart attack two weeks earlier, and Ember, a college friend, and I would be singing an additional tribute in memory of his father during the wedding service. Having heard the news on the way to the rehearsal, I was bracing myself and praying the Lord would give me discernment on what to say, if anything, in order to comfort the family. Little did I know how much the Pearson family would speak to me.

Throughout the weekend, I was amazed at the strength, composure, and relentless devotion to Christ exhibited by the Pearson family. During the rehearsal dinner, two events remain etched on the backdrop of my brain: Mrs. Pearson's blessing and Paul's heartfelt plea. Mrs. Pearson stood before a hundred people or so and read a blessing to Erin and Paul, which she wrote on the morning of her husband's death. The blessing was beautifully written, in particular the end, which continues to resonate in my ears. Over and over again she commanded her son to leave her. She stressed the importance of Paul's role as Erin's husband and understood the necessity of leaving and cleaving. I was amazed at her strength. Later I spoke to her about her toast in more detail, and she just felt an overwhelming need to make sure Paul understood the Lord would take care of her and that he needed to start his own family. She and her departed husband gave Paul permission to start his life, free from guilt. What a woman of God!

In the same vein, it is said that challenges reveal one's character. I sat amazed as Paul addressed the wedding party. The person who stood before me was a man, solidified by fire. He spoke about his father who was revered by the community. A father of six, a loving husband, and an active member in the Texas community ... yet, Paul's message was simple. The good my father did was because of Christ. You didn't love my father; you loved Christ in him. Even at his death, the Gospel was preached. Although I never met Paul's dad, it was apparent his legacy of Christian service would be continued through his children, who love Christ with passion and vigor even during challenging circumstances.

For many young couples, challenging circumstances revolve around miscarriages. Last year some friends of mine miscarried their first child; and then their second son was born prematurely (nearly two months), weighing in at three pounds and dropped down to two pounds and six ounces before gaining weight. Needless to say, this young couple has experienced more trials than most as first-time parents. Yet, read the following excerpt from my friend. What a remarkable witness in the face of adversity. He truly embodies the verse: "Consider it pure joy, my brothers, whenever you face trials of many kinds, because you know that the testing of your faith develops perseverance. Perseverance must finish its work so that you may be mature and complete, not lacking anything" (James 1:2-4).

> Thanks so much for your prayers!!! When I was at the hospital this morning, a nurse [not his regular nurse—never seen her before] was holding Alexander. Typically, I place a hand on him in his crib while praying. Since she was holding him, I just held his tiny hand and prayed. When I was done, the nurse said, "That's the best medicine he can get." I was able to testify to the fact that he's done so well in comparison to all the babies around us because of the countless prayers that have been lifted up for him … and she actually understood this fact and acknowledged it! It's always comforting to meet others who believe in Jesus! Alexander's situation has provided great opportunities for me to testify of God's grace and goodness … so as you pray for Alexander, also praise God for the opportunities He's given me to share Him with others!!! Thanks again for your prayers!

Even in the face of adversity, he praises the God of all creation and looks for opportunities to share the Good News with others. You'll be happy to know little Alexander is happy, healthy, and expecting a sibling anytime now. May we all embrace our trials as learning opportunities, knowing that "the Lord is good, a refuge in times of trouble. He cares for those who trust in Him" (Nah. 1:7). Let us be legacies for Christ. Let us allow Christ to work through us so that others might be drawn to the well where the water never runs dry.

Seasoned Advice

Dr. Joe White, 55, president of Kanakuk Kamps and founder of Kids Across America, Branson, Missouri: Football at Southern Methodist University was a challenging, but rich and rewarding experience. During my junior year at SMU, I was fortunate to be able to marry a wonderful young lady and enjoy fourteen months together as husband and wife. After graduating SMU, I moved to College Station, Texas, where I began coaching college football at Texas A&M University. It was on the evening of the first spring practice that my wife informed me that she no longer was in love with me and instead was in love with a good friend of mine. When she moved back to her home the next morning, the sickening sense of sadness in my heart was indescribable. The next three months of my life were months of almost unbearable pain. I've never blamed my ex-wife for her actions or found fault in my heart with my friend, who later married her. There was never vengeance or blame.

Somehow during those three months of intense grief, the One who wrote "Yea, though I walk through the valley of the shadow of death, I will fear no evil, for Thou art with me, Thy rod and Thy staff, they comfort me" met me in that valley. It was definitely the valley, of the shadow of death, but it was definitely the perfect prescription for my needs. During my days in that valley a lot of pride inside of me died. A lot of my self-serving ego died. There was a scar put in my heart that provided me the necessary trust that would carry me through a lifetime of service.

Though I "walked with a limp," the limp is the most welcome part of my body. As I look back upon these days of tragedy, I can honestly say they were the most significant days of my life. It was during my time in that valley that my heart was born again with a love for God that I had never experienced before. During those deep, dark days in the valley, I was on the surgeon's table, and He was using His scalpel to give me open-heart surgery and placed a new heart in me that loved Him more than I was ever

40

CHARACTER

capable of loving Him before.

You see, it is only in "dying" that we are "born" into eternal life. Galatians 2:20 has become a theme for me, and thankfully, the tragedy gave the theme life in my mortal bones. "I have been crucified with Christ. It is no longer I who live, but Christ who lives in me. The life I live, I live by faith in the Son of God, who died for me and gave Himself up for me."

As the months went by, God in His loving kindness was great enough to introduce me to the love of my lifetime, Debbie Jo, who has become my wife and mother of my four kids. I've never loved anyone the way I love Debbie Jo. God is definitely a God of second chances. I feel like I have married way over my head, and don't understand how a woman as amazing as she is could love a wounded soldier like me. But if a princess can kiss the frog, then I suppose this princess can love a frog like me!

God is definitely the God who puts the beautiful snow-capped mountain peaks just on the other side of the lethal valley of failure. As the Apostle Paul (my hero) writes in Philippians 3:7-11, his words have become my lifeblood. "Whatever things were gain to me, those things I count as loss for the sake of Christ. More than that, I have counted all things to be loss in view of the surpassing value of knowing Christ Jesus my Lord, for whom I have suffered the loss of all things, and count them but rubbish so that I may gain Christ, and may be found in Him, not having a righteousness of my own derived from the Law, but that which is through faith in Christ, the righteousness which comes from God on the basis of faith, that I may know Him, and the power of His resurrection and the fellowship of His sufferings, being conformed to His death; in order that I may attain the resurrection from the dead" (NAS).

Doug Birnie, 49, area development director, Focus on the Family, Colorado Springs, Colorado: A week ago I took my daughter Dana to a John Maxwell leadership event that featured a full day of impressive speakers. My main motivation in taking Dana was to introduce her to John Wooden, the legendary basketball coach. After Coach Wooden spoke, John Maxwell asked him a number of questions, the last one being: "What do you want your legacy to be?" Coach Wooden's answer was simple and straightforward. He said that he did not want to be known as a basketball coach who won a lot of championships but that he really wanted to be remembered as a man who was considerate of others. I was sitting next to his daughter, and when her dad said that, she nodded her head slightly and with a tear in her eye said, "He really is such a good man."

My own answer would incorporate Coach Wooden's. Jesus told us that we are to love others as we love ourselves. However, I would take it a step further. As Christians, I believe we are called to bring others into a relationship with Jesus. Therefore, while I want to be considerate of others, it's more important that my motivation for doing so serves the purpose of letting people see Jesus's love through me. Overall, I want to be remembered as a man who was intent on living the life that God wanted me to live. Ideally, I want to die to self and live for Christ.

Points to Ponder

1. How have your adversities shaped you?

2. If you could, what would you do differently during the process?

3. What would you tell a friend going through a similar adversity?

4. What do you desire your legacy to be?

WHAT IS THE SECRET TO DETERMINING GOD'S WILL?

"I believe a man does what he can until his destiny is revealed." —*The Last Samurai*

Determining God's will for our lives remains a central focus for many of our waking hours, intentionally or unintentionally. As children, we attempt many different activities, quickly discerning those in which we excel and those in which we do not. In high school, we begin to build on our strengths, only to start all over again in college trying to ascertain the direction of our careers. When I worked in admissions at a major university, nearly 40 percent of all incoming freshmen declared Pre-Med as their major. By the end of their sophomore year, the number fell to 17 percent due to the realities of expectations placed upon them. Many young people feel the pressure to be someone they are not in order to please others.

The truth is that each of us has God's will for our lives written into our being. The Psalmist says, "I praise you because I am fearfully and wonderfully made; your works are wonderful, I know that full well. My frame was not hidden from you when I was made in the secret place. When I was woven together in the depths of the earth, your eyes saw my unformed body. All the days ordained for me were written in your book before one of them came to be" (Ps. 139:14-16). In many ways our lives mirror a game of chess; at each moment we attempt to make the best choice with the knowledge we have. Often, we may have appeared to make the wrong choice, but God's vantage point differs from ours; he sees the big picture. As long as we learn from every experience and remain obedient to the impressions God places on our hearts, we cannot fail. Ultimately, every experience potentially prepares us for something wonderful the Lord has in store for us.

For instance, at the ripe age of seventeen, Joseph dreamed his brothers would some day bow before him (Gen. 37:5-7). As you can imagine, this did not go over too well with his older brothers, who already perceived Joseph as their father's favorite, so they plotted to kill him. Fortunately for Joseph, they ended up selling him to the Ishmaelites instead. Over the years, the Lord took Joseph down many different difficult roads, all of which helped develop his character and reliance on God, culminating with the interpretation of Pharaoh's haunting dreams: "'I cannot do it,' Joseph replied to Pharaoh, 'but God will give Pharaoh the answer he desires'" (Gen. 41:16). In all situations, Joseph chose to give God all the honor and glory. As a result, after Joseph interpreted Pharaoh's dream, Pharaoh recognized that Joseph's wisdom came directly from God and placed the whole land of Egypt under his charge (Gen. 41:39-40). In the end, during the great famine, his brothers came to him pleading for sustenance. After sending them away a few times, he ultimately wept before his brothers and told them, "Do not be angry with yourselves for selling me here, because it was to save lives that God sent me ahead of you" (Gen. 45:5).

In the case of Joseph, the Lord needed to teach him many lessons before he would be ready to assume his place in history. The same could be said for each of us. In order for us to assume our place in history, the Lord desires our obedience. In our obedience, His plan for our lives will be revealed: "He guides the humble [obedient] in what is right and teaches them in his way" (Ps. 25:9). We may not know what the future holds for our lives, but God calls us to a life of obedience today.

↗ ↙ ↗ ↙ ↗

Seasoned Advice

Raymond C. Walker, 52, president of The Walker Companies, Atlanta, Georgia: As a college student in the late '60s/early '70s, a dramatic shift occurred in terms of what our generation considered acceptable thought and behavior. I was a product of that shift. Never being taught the Gospel of Christ (even though my family conveyed a shallow acceptance), my foundation for learning and growing was almost completely secular. I remember reading Ayn Rand and Marshall McLuhan in college and being captivated by modern existentialism ... we are "nothing more than our experiences" ... selfish "individualism" was the only formula for real joy and satisfaction in the world. This mindset carried over into my twenties. Upon graduating from college, my focus was almost completely on self-centered pursuits—career, money, status, adventure, and romance. These were the benchmarks of my happiness and, to a large extent, our culture then and now. Despite much success, I was always "running," and the victories never seemed to satisfy the demands of my mind and heart.

It wasn't until my late thirties that God literally beat me to my knees. I had started a business in the summer of 1987 (sixty days before the stock market crashed). After hanging on by a thread for more than two years, the first Gulf War broke out; the Savings and Loan crises caused a dramatic recession; and my youngest son (Ryan), who had not spoken a word in three years, was diagnosed as autistic. There was no way I could solve any of this. So after castigating organized religion for most of my adult life, I dropped down beside my bed and prayed to a God I knew nothing about. I made a genuine and earnest effort to grow spiritually … regular church, tithing, Bible study, and prayer. I read everything I could get my hands on that might help me understand Truth. It was a terribly slow but steady process … after several years, I asked Christ to save me and come into my life, and nothing has been the same since. God faithfully revealed Himself, and tossed in more than one miracle along the way … including my son's complete healing.

So what does all this say to those twentysomethings who are trying to find their way? It is simple, maybe trite. Do not allow this materialistic culture to undermine your commitment to love God with all your heart, mind, and strength. You will naturally have strong urges to make money, find a mate, cut loose, etc. This is "the season" for some of these things in your life, however, never lose sight of the *main* thing: Cultivate your faith and believe *completely* in God's economy and time.

In my case, I had to extricate myself from more than one cul de sac, back up, reassess, redirect, and patiently endure. It was painful and unnecessary. My priorities have been completely recast, and my confidence in God's plan has never been greater. Get those priorities in line and patiently let your life unfold. With prayerful thought and reflection, you all probably know the right "next steps" in your life plan. It does not have to be grandiose or dramatic. The bottom line is to follow the path that you know keeps you in God's will. Ignore all the external pressure or internal anxiety that causes uncertainty and conflict … just follow the Lord!

Linda Wharton, 52, division president, Rels Settlement Services, Bloomington, Minnesota: I married very young (eighteen). My husband and I did not have children until I was twenty-two. That is young in today's world, but thirty years ago that was okay. I had my second child at twenty-six. My plan was always to be a wife and mother. My mother was a stay-at-home mom and raised ten kids. I felt I had had the best possible teacher and that God had given me two wonderful children to provide a good home for. Well, their father had different plans. He chose to live a different life and one day left to start that life. I had no job and even less confidence. I looked at those two kids and knew that God really did mean for me to take care of them. I was just not planning on taking care of them the way this was turning out. Funny how He sometimes changes our plans! He provided me with the most wonderful network of friends and support people. He really did know what He was doing from the beginning. Today, those kids are two very happy and successful young men. My life has been very rewarding and fulfilling. He opened so many doors when He closed that one more than twenty years ago. His grace is awesome.

Points to Ponder

1. How is God calling you to a life of obedience today?

2. Do you feel as though God has abandoned you? If so, how?

3. Map out the major experiences of your life on a piece of paper. Next to each one, write down what you have learned from each experience.

IS FELLOWSHIP
A PRIORITY
FOR YOU?

"Christian brotherhood is not an ideal which we must realize; it is rather a reality created by God in Christ in which we may participate. The more clearly we learn to recognize that the ground and strength and promise of all our fellowship is in Jesus Christ alone, the more serenely shall we think of our fellowship and pray and hope for it."[1]
—Dietrich Bonhoeffer, *Life Together*

↗ ↙ ↗ ↙ ↗

A few months ago, two of my dear friends emailed to ask for prayer. Both of these young men had lost a grandfather. Their families wrestled with the loss of an important person within their community. We're all drawn to communities of people, aren't we? We all want to belong. I think that is one reason why the Internet has been so successful: People want to be known. We desire to be around those individuals who know and love us for who we are and not necessarily for anything we may do for them. Unfortunately, with greater demands on our time, we substitute television relationships for intimacy. For instance, the earth stood still in spring of 2004 as *Friends* went off the air. More than 40 million Americans hovered around their television sets to say goodbye to their buddies. In *USA Today*, Linda Kaplan Thaler calls these compressed experiences "McMoments—compact, tailor-made mini-experiences that perfectly fit the temporal contours of our daily lives, with no assembly required. Instead of actually spending a leisurely night out with real friends, we depend on six strangers to do the work for us, enjoying their strong bonds of intimacy and sharing their never-ending romantic adventures. And all in less than 30 minutes."[2] Time inevitably drives wedges between communities unless communities are cared for consistently. I have been blessed with many communities in my life, but one always remains central to my heart, Chi Rho (Christian Men's Acappella Ensemble of Wake Forest University).

"See you again next year" remarked one friend as others reciprocated … even though we knew we would see each other before then. The statement, though, solidified a commitment to one another and to a common mission.

Following Chi Rho's Ninth Annual Big Concert, we were the last ones out of the New Village Tavern on Saturday night. None of us wanted to leave. Contentment laced our conversation or rather laced our tales of yesteryear. Friendships rooted in service to Christ. Friendships ordained by God. Friendships bronzed in the trenches of ministry.

For many of us, as years multiply since college, our time spent in ministry with brothers in Chi Rho remains our fondest. As I reflected about the evening with a friend later that night, he drew a parallel to heaven: "As we swapped stories, I had an overwhelming sense of contentment as if there was no place on earth that I would rather be. I think that's how heaven will be." Fellowship gives us a snapshot of how heaven might be, "for where two or three come together in my name, there am I with them" (Matthew 18:20). There is a misconception among Christians that one must be praying or studying God's Word in order to achieve fellowship, "but if we walk in the light, as he is in the light, we have fellowship with one another, and the blood of Jesus, his Son, purifies us from all sin" (1 John 1:7). Fellowship with other believers is so integral to our spiritual development.

For most of us, true fellowship began in college. College is such a unique time because fellowship and community come so easily. During our tenure at college there was an abundance of fellowship opportunities. Thus, in the spring of my junior year, when a friend, Brittany, assembled a small group of us to pray for her new fellowship vision at our college, I thought to myself … why do we need another fellowship group here on campus? I still remember going into her dorm room with six to eight other people when Brittany, with her sparkling eyes and toothy smile, reached underneath her bed and pulled out a poster she had made. To this day, I still chuckle every time I think of this poster. She had hundreds of faces, no arms, no legs, just faces. At the top of the poster were faces with guitars, drums and musical notes. She longed to reach more of the fraternity and sorority crowd by having students lead students in worship and teaching. We prayed for a few months until Brittany decided it was time to have our first meeting in Davis Chapel. She asked a friend and me to lead music. I have always loved singing, but at this stage in my life I had just started playing the guitar … I was not good. In spite of the worship, God moved through people's hearts because they desired community. They longed to fellowship with Christ. They longed to fill a void in their hearts. Soon after, Student to Student (STS) moved into a larger venue to accommodate the hundreds of people who were drawn to this ministry. As the ministry grew, God raised others up who were more talented than I, so I could move aside. STS continues to meet on Wednesday nights at 10:00. It is considered a sacred time.

As Christians, we are designed to live in community: "And let us consider how we may spur one another on toward love and good deeds. Let us not give up meeting together, as some are in the habit of doing, but let us encourage one another—all the more as you see the Day approaching" (Hebrews 10:24-25). It is critical for you to find an affinity group of some sort, a group of people who will pray, support, exhort, and challenge you to be God's man or woman on a daily basis. We are designed to live in communities; don't settle for "McMoments."

⤢ ⤡ ⤢ ⤡ ⤢

Seasoned Advice

Victoria Jackson, 45, actress, formerly of *Saturday Night Live*, Los Angeles, California—My twenties were very exciting. The month I turned twenty, I left my home in Miami, Florida, and moved to Los Angeles to be an actress. After a few years of doing odd jobs and a ten-minute stand-up comedy act that I wrote myself, I ended up on *The Tonight Show with Johnny Carson*. That was my big break. Three years later, an audition led to a cast-member spot on *Saturday Night Live*, where I enjoyed six stress-filled but amazing years. I got married, had my first baby in my twenties and made a lot of money. The only thing I did wrong was let my relationship with Christ slip from the number-one spot to the number-two spot, and He won't stand for that.

Having no money and no family in LA, I struggled to find myself a job and a safe, cheap apartment and an affordable car. Those were my priorities instead of finding a church. I'd grown up in a Christian home and attended church my whole life and Florida Bible College for a year. I thought, "I know every verse in the Bible; I can find a church anytime. Rent and food and a job are more important right now." That was my big mistake. Because I had no Christian fellowship, I started hanging out with people from my secular jobs, and after a few years didn't think drinking and smoking were so shocking. As a lonely twenty-two-year-old Baptist virgin, I started a relationship with

a promiscuous non-Christian even though I heard God whisper-
ing loudly in my ear, "Be ye not unequally yoked together with
unbelievers: for what fellowship hath light with darkness" (2 Cor.
6:14 KJV). I did start attending church with him, and we ended
up getting married, and he eventually professed faith in Christ,
but is now into New Age and other strange things. My seven
years of marriage to him were sad and lonely. I ended up paying him alimony for six years, losing all my *SNL* earnings, and
having to see my baby Scarlet go through a divorce. God forgave
me for disobeying Him, but I still had to pay the consequences.
God's mercy kept me from getting any diseases from this man.
I have now been married 12 years to a great Christian man who
happens to be my high school sweetheart, my first love. We
have two beautiful daughters, Scarlet and Aubrey, and we are a
very happy family. God is our number-one 1 priority, and our
first consideration in every decision. I'm mostly a mom but do
TV jobs and stand-up comedy here and there. I've just started
doing some public speaking, giving my testimony. My only
advice to twenty-year-olds is to follow your dreams, your passion,
but to keep God first. He forgives, but He wants to bless us so
much, and we shouldn't get in the way of His goodness. When
He's speaking to you, listen and obey, or you'll have to pay the
consequences: "Delight yourself also in the Lord, and He shall
give you the desires of your heart. Commit your way to the Lord,
trust also in Him, and He shall bring it to pass" (Ps. 37:4-5
NKJV). To summarize all my thoughts, if I had to leave twenty-
year-olds with one thing, it would be this: "This Book of the Law
shall not depart from your mouth, but you shall meditate in it
day and night, that you may observe to do according to all that
is written in it. For then you will make your way prosperous, and
then you will have good success. Have I not commanded you? Be
strong and of good courage; do not be afraid, nor be dismayed,
for the Lord your God is with you wherever you go" (Josh. 1:8-9
NKJV).

Points to Ponder

1. Are you in a community right now?

2. If not, what is keeping you from being in a community?

3. Who encourages you? How so?

1. Dietrich Bonhoeffer, *Life Together* (HarperCollins Publishers, NY, NY: 1954) p. 30.
2. Linda Kaplan Thaler, "'Friends' Finale Exposes Culture of McMoments" (*USA Today*, May 3, 2004).

WILL GOD REALLY BRING ME A SPOUSE?

I fully believe God fulfills the desires of our hearts: "Delight thyself also in the Lord; and he shall give thee the desires of thine heart" (Ps. 37:4 KJV), "Wait for the Lord; be strong and take heart and wait for the Lord" (Ps. 27:14), and "May he give you the desire of your heart and make all your plans succeed" (Ps. 20:4). One of my greatest desires—serving alongside my wife in building a Christian home—has yet to be realized. Ironically enough, at times I feel as though God has used me in preparing others for marriage through roommates and girls whom I've dated. Allow me to elaborate.

When I first moved to Atlanta, I warned my friend that my last four roommates had all gotten engaged after living with me. He failed to heed my warning. Later that spring, after dating a lovely young lady for approximately three months, he

55

got engaged and they wed six months later. Last year, I never "officially" dated a colleague, but we spent a good deal of time together cultivating a friendship over the school year. After a few months, she ended up going back to her high school sweetheart for whom the torch had never faded. Yes, I have the innate ability to drive people to marriage. I am always the last person they date or the last roommate they have before they get engaged: five roommates, seven girlfriends, and I've been in twenty-five wedding parties. As you might imagine, it is a source of amusement for many of my friends.

At times it is difficult to understand why some are blessed with a spouse while others are not. Often one begins to question, "What is wrong with me? Am I not devoted enough to God for Him to bless me? Am I not pretty enough? Am I not smart enough? What's wrong with me?" Some days are definitely more challenging than others, but your trust must remain in the ultimate gift-giver. Do you believe God's promises? Is He perfect? Is He infallible? Do you truly believe that He "knows the plans [he has] for you," and that He "plans to prosper you and not to harm you, plans to give you hope and a future" (Jer. 29:11). Do you believe the Psalmist's words, when he says, "For you created my inmost being; you knit me together in my mother's womb. I praise you because I am fearfully and wonderfully made; your works are wonderful, I know that full well. My frame was not hidden from you when I was made in the secret place. When I was woven together in the depths of the earth, your eyes saw my unformed body. All the days ordained for me were written in your book before one of them came to be" (Ps. 139:13-16). I'm so thankful the Lord knows what is best for us. His way of answering prayers may not always be our heart's desire at that time, but never doubt that God desires His best for you. Garth Brooks' "Unanswered Prayers" says it best:

> She was the one that I'd wanted for all times
> And each night I'd spend prayin' that God would make her mine
> And if He'd only grant me this wish I wished back then

I'd never ask for anything again
Sometimes I thank God for unanswered prayers
Remember when you're talkin' to the man upstairs
That just because He doesn't answer doesn't mean He don't care
Some of God's greatest gifts are unanswered prayers

Recently, I felt like I was living the lyrics to this song. Just the other night, I saw my college sweetheart whom I thought I would marry. We hadn't seen each other for four or five years. She's married now, pregnant, and very happy. I was grateful for her happiness as well as God's impeccable wisdom to know that we were not meant for each other. We think we know what is best for us, but God knows our needs, our wants, and our heart's desires because He "is able to do immeasurably more than all we ask or imagine, according to his power that is at work within us" (Eph. 3:20). Waiting, at times, is difficult, but we need to be faithful as He is faithful to us. In his book, *Fresh Faith*, Jim Cymbala said, "The hardest part of faith is often simply to wait. And the trouble is, if we don't, then we start to fix the problem ourselves—and that makes it worse. We complicate the situation to the point where it takes God much longer to fix it than if we had quietly waited for His working in the first place."[1]

Singleness is a trying time for many, but I cling to the idea that God is sovereign. Jim Elliot resigned his life to whatever would give God the most glory. Ultimately, his death gave God the most glory because thousands, if not millions, of young people became missionaries looking to Jim as a shining example of devoting their lives to Christ. The following poem (author unknown) always evokes a tremendous response whenever I share it with people. It speaks to my heart on the notion of waiting on God.

Wait

Desperately, helplessly, longingly, I cried:
Quietly, patiently, lovingly God replied.

I pled and I wept for a clue to my fate,
And the Master so gently said, "Child, you must wait."

"Wait? You say, wait!" my indignant reply.
"Lord, I need answers, I need to know why!
Is your hand shortened? Or have You not heard?
By Faith, I have asked, and am claiming your Word.

My future and all to which I can relate
Hangs in the balance, and YOU tell me to WAIT?
I'm needing a 'yes,' a go-ahead sign,
Or even a 'no' to which I can resign.

And Lord, You promised that if we believe
We need but to ask, and we shall receive.
And Lord, I've been asking, and this is my cry:
I'm weary of asking! I need a reply!"

Then quietly, softly, I learned of my fate
As my Master replied once again, "You must wait."

So, I slumped in my chair, defeated and taut
And grumbled to God, "So, I'm waiting … for what?"

He seemed, then, to kneel, and His eyes wept with mine,
And He tenderly said, "I could give you a sign.
I could shake the heavens, and darken the sun.
I could raise the dead, and cause mountains to run.

All you seek, I could give, and pleased you would be.
You would have what you want—But, you wouldn't know Me.

You'd not know the depth of My love for each saint;
You'd not know the power that I give to the faint;
You'd not learn to see through the clouds of despair;
You'd not learn to trust just by knowing I'm there;

You'd not know the joy of resting in Me
When darkness and silence were all you could see.
You'd never experience that fullness of love
As the peace of My Spirit descends like a dove;
You'd know that I give and I save ... (for a start),
But you'd not know the depth of the beat of My heart.

The glow of My comfort late into the night,
The faith that I give when you walk without sight,
The depth that's beyond getting just what you asked
Of an infinite God, who makes what you have LAST.

You'd never know, should your pain quickly flee,
What it means that 'My grace is sufficient for Thee.'
Yes, your dreams for your loved one overnight would come true,
But, Oh, the Loss! If I lost what I'm doing in you!

So, be silent, My child, and in time you will see
That the greatest of gifts is to get to know Me.
And though oft' may My answers seem terribly late,
My most precious answer of all is still, 'WAIT.'"

↗ ↙ ↗ ↙ ↗

Seasoned Advice

Mike Edens, 48, occupational health professional, Winston-Salem, North Carolina: One of my best recollections of my later twenties, had to do with my marriage and family planning. My wife, Mary Beth, and I met when I was a senior in college and she was a sophomore. We enjoyed a fun, typical, collegiate dating experience for a year, but then embarked on another four years of long-distance dating. Mary Beth had had a relationship with Christ for a number of years before we met, but I had only really become a Christian in my senior year of college. Our toughest couple of years were when I went off to graduate school in Alabama and she was still in school in North Carolina. I had a strong sense that God was using this time and distance to grow me as a spiritual leader if we were to get married. I learned in this experience to trust in God to preserve the relationship if it was meant to be. My nature would have been to be jealous of Mary Beth dating others while still a college student. The fact that God gave me such peace about her completing her college experience, even if that meant dating other guys, was evidence to me that God was in the relationship. I believe this had a lot to do with preserving the relationship.

Points to Ponder

1. Read Psalm 139.

2. Do you believe in God's promises?

3. Do you believe God has your best interest at heart? If so, how?

4. Do you believe the God of details doesn't know what He's doing? Explain to God why you are frustrated or upset.

1. Jim Cymbala, *Fresh Faith* (Zondervan, Grand Rapids, MI: 1999) p. 111.

read to me in her rocking chair; as an adolescent she would bring home sample textbooks from school, like *Rainbows* and *Moonbeams*. I loved all sorts of books, but I preferred non-fiction, especially biographies. Ordinary men achieving great feats have always brought tears to my eyes. The Bible is laced with ordinary men accomplishing monumental feats, such as David over Goliath or twelve regular men who changed the world.

After college, in order to compensate for not attending church until high school, I voraciously read the Bible and Christian literature. I often would read a book or two a week. As a teacher with new responsibilities, I have slowed down, but still reap the fruits of a discipline I started many years ago. A friend of mine told me that whenever he read an excerpt in a book he liked, he would make a vertical slash along the margins. Then, he would write the page number in the back sleeve with a word or two about the content. This practice has paid numerous dividends through the years whenever I'm asked to give a talk/devotion, write, or encourage a friend. How many times do you remember reading some great principle but not being able to find the quotation? Trust me, this system works well. In addition, for the last eight years I have sent out a weekly encouraging email to friends and family. The majority of those emails have consisted of short excerpts from books that I am reading. My filing system has made this exercise virtually painless.

In short, books are wonderful tools for growth, but always be analytical in your reading. Measure the words you read against the Word of God: "For the word of God is living and active. Sharper than any double-edged sword, it penetrates even to dividing soul and spirit, joints and marrow; it judges the thoughts and attitudes of the heart" (Heb. 4:12).

↗ ↙ ↗ ↙ ↗

Seasoned Advice

Ravi Zacharias, 58, Ravi Zacharias International Ministries, Norcross, Georgia: If I had even the faintest clue when I was younger as to how profound an impact books and professors would have upon my life, I would have kept a better record of my thoughts and emotions. Why? Because some books and teachers leave their indelible fingerprints on our souls. A book

by Leonard Ravenhill is the first that shaped me beyond any dispute (outside of the Scriptures) and probably more dramatically than any other book I have read. An English revivalist born in 1907, Ravenhill wrote several books on the theme of prayer and revival, and *Why Revival Tarries* is the volume that impacted me.[1] From page after page, I made notes and wrote down what Leonard Ravenhill was saying. I got his tapes on prayer and revival and would listen to them at home. I still remember my mother asking, "Aren't you tired of that man's voice? Night after night you're hearing his voice. It's echoing through these walls." That was the effect the book was having on me; I couldn't get enough.

Among the thoughts that shaped me most was the story Ravenhill told of the notorious British criminal Charlie Peace, who was going to his death on a capital offense. As the minister was reading from the Bible and another book, Charlie Peace asked him, "Do you really believe in such a place called hell?" The minister replied, "Yes." Charlie responded—and this is the thought that impacted me—"Sir, if I believed what you and the church of God say that you believe, even if England were covered with broken glass from coast to coast, I would walk over it, if need be, on hands and knees, and think it worthwhile living, just to save one soul from an eternal hell like that!"[2] That struck me. If what we lay claim to on these matters is true, then the dramatic influence in our lives is going to be inestimable. "Even if England were covered with broken glass from coast to coast, I would walk over it." That is the kind of reality and these are the words that shape one's call. This was the truth I was going to proclaim. Ravenhill was a fire-and-brimstone preacher, no doubt about it. When I read him today, I wonder, "Will today's audience really listen to this kind of teaching?" But there was a time for him; there was an anointing upon him and a mission for him.

And for me, *Why Revival Tarries* sealed my call to preach and proclaim, and it convinced me that this was a real message. I was not going to shirk from whatever sacrifice was required to take this message to the world. Little did I know that God was going to enable me to do just that. Such is the value of a good book, and I commend good reading to all young men and women who wish to serve God with a full heart and mind.

Points to Ponder

1. Take a look at your bookshelf today.
   Do the books and magazines you own accurately reflect what's important to you?

2. Consider re-reading your favorite book.

3. What book has been the most influential in your life?
   Tell a friend why this book is so important to you.

1. Leonard Ravenhill, *Why Revival Tarries* (Minneapolis, Minn.: Bethany Fellowship, 1959).
2. Ibid., 19.

HOW DO
YOU COMBAT
APATHY?

The day after Thanksgiving my sister came with her family to visit us in Chicago. My niece, Bella, continues to emulate her mother, while my nephew, Gibson, idolizes me. Just kidding, of course. Gibson is about two-and-a-half years old and practices talking by mimicking everything others say. While I was showing him the fascinating mechanics of the reclining chair, I noticed an accumulation of food particles in the hidden pouch component. My immediate reaction was, "That's disgusting," followed by Gibson's echo, "That's disgusting." We then continued the same routine over and over again. Gibson would use all of his weight to pull out the extension to the chair, point, smile, and say, "That's disgusting," slight head turn to judge my reaction, followed by his attempt to push the chair back together. During one attempt, he pushed, grimaced, stopped, and turned to me

67

and said, "Please help me." My heart melted. I love the inno-
cence of children; not only was Gibson willing to ask for help,
but he also had complete trust that all he had to do was ask.

Turning to and trusting in God isn't always our immediate
response when faced with adversity. More specifically, remaining
obedient to God's Word and faithful to His promises, at times,
proves dauntingly difficult. Most of us fall victim to apathy in
our relationship with God if we are honest with ourselves. Having been a Christian for a while now, fighting apathy has gotten
harder and harder because acting on my feelings comes more
naturally than acting on what I know. In Revelations 3:16, it
states, "So, because you are lukewarm—neither hot nor cold—I
am about to spit you out of my mouth." What do you do when
you just don't feel like spending time with God?

By no means am I an expert on this subject, nor do I claim to
have the catch-all answer; all I can offer are the outpourings of
my experiences. After much reflection, I have concluded that my
apathy stems from two major areas: busyness and boredom.

Busyness:
• Boundaries are critical in order to guard your time with
God. For example, I know certain individuals who simply never
return emails. Personally, this drives me crazy, but it shackles the
tyranny of the urgent for these men. Others never bring work
home. Still others keep the Sabbath holy regardless of the situation. If every moment of your day is scheduled, how and when
does God lead you?

• Maintaining discipline in the midst of busyness also proves
challenging. Habits take three weeks to form and moments to
break. Disobedience starts small. Our school enforces our dress
code because we are attempting to teach if you are faithful in the
small things, you will remain faithful in the larger things. Never
give Satan a foothold for "whoever shall keep the whole law, and
yet stumble in one point is guilty of all" (James 2:10).

• Disobedience in the small things tends to lead to a downward spiral of shame. Oswald Chambers said, "There is only one

way by which I can get right with God, and that is through the death of Jesus Christ. I must get rid of the underlying idea that I can ever be right with God because of my obedience. Who of us could ever obey God to absolute perfection!"[1]

Boredom:

• Failure to see God's blessings on a daily basis results in boredom with life or belief that God is not as "real" in society today. For many years I followed a practice, which I still occasionally repeat. Bill Hybels, in *Too Busy Not to Pray*, advocates a prayer method, which I've found is excellent in seeing God's blessings in your life. Hybels writes out his prayers daily on one sheet of paper under the ACTS method – Adoration, Confession, Thanksgiving, and Supplication; one page forces brevity and focus of thoughts.[2] Systematically every few weeks, I would flip through the pages and place a star next to all the answered prayers. Oftentimes, we pray for one thing and then the next, without giving thanks for the prayers that have been answered.

• Scripture memory is an excellent way to keep your mind focused on godly things: "I have hidden your word in my heart that I might not sin against you" (Ps. 119:11). Our thought life can be extremely damaging to our relationship with God, thus "We demolish arguments and every pretension that sets itself up against the knowledge of God, and we take captive every thought to make it obedient to Christ" (2 Cor. 10:5).

• Switch up your quiet times. Try something new and different. For those of you who know me or have lived with me, I love to sing. Singing praises to the Lord brings me extreme joy. Another friend of mine walks around in order to keep himself from falling asleep. Be creative. God wired each person differently for a reason.

• Finally, I think boredom with life in general can creep in if you are not careful. A friend of mine talks about how too many young people are concerned with having "exciting" jobs, when in reality they need to bring excitement to their jobs. Unfortunately, dashed dreams and unrealized expectations are a part of life, but over time dwelling on "what could have been" leaves you lonely and depressed.

What do you do when you just don't feel like spending time with God? Much like an athlete in training, you push through the pain: "No, I beat my body and make it my slave so that after I have preached to others, I myself will not be disqualified for the prize" (1 Cor. 9:27).

↗ ↙ ↗ ↙ ↗

Seasoned Advice

Elinor Starling, 69, grandmother, Winston-Salem, North Carolina: Having lived through these last years and seen the changes that have taken place in society and are continuing to take place, I fully understand the value of having a firm foundation in Christian values. One of the best pieces of advice I can give is to never be satisfied with where you are in your Christian life. Don't think that just by attending church you will be secure in resisting all the temptations that the world has to offer. Society throws some very enticing things our way. Learning to discern what is good and what is not is a constant challenge.

I am a voracious reader and have spent many hours reading some of the trustworthy Christian apologists and writers of today as well as from the past to help me sharpen my discerning skills. Several that have been most helpful are Francis Schaeffer, Ravi Zacharias, R.C. Sproul, James Kennedy, John Piper, J.I. Packer, Charles Colson, Sinclair Ferguson, and Robert Godfrey. There are many others too numerous to mention, but resources are available on most any issue. I believe that Christians must keep our eyes open and ears alert to see and understand the important issues of the day. Then we need to speak out and be ready to fight. And, most important, we have to keep our eyes fixed on Jesus and be obedient to Him. We are in a race, and it is a marathon not a sprint! Don't stop defending the faith. We want to be able to say with Paul, "I have fought the good fight, I have finished the race, I have kept the faith" (2 Tim. 4:7).

Points to Ponder

1. Is there a cycle to when you don't feel like spending time with God?

2. Think back to precious times with the Lord. What made those times so special?

3. Write a letter to yourself reminding yourself all the reasons why you love the Lord. Place it in your Bible for those times when you don't feel like spending time with God.

FROZEN
BY FEAR?

One night after I first moved to Atlanta, I had just turned out my light, and I was ready to go to bed. Then suddenly, I heard a loud BANG. In most neighborhoods, this would be cause for alarm, but I didn't live in the best part of town. You see, a few days earlier I had heard gunshots, bottle rockets had hit my window … so a bang didn't affect me very much. After a few minutes though, I noticed it was getting hot in my room. Glancing up at my ceiling fan, I noticed it had stopped, so I concluded the power must be off. My imagination started to create crazy scenarios. Thus, I hopped out of bed and walked to my bedroom door. As I was reaching for the doorknob, BANG BANG BANG BANG BANG BANG. Fearlessly, I threw the door open and pounded on my roommate's door, shouting, "Kevin … Kevin." Well, it took him awhile to wake up. As I was explaining the situation, there was a thumping on our front door. We fumbled our way to the door, glanced through the peephole and slowly opened the door. There stood some guy named Bubba, who said, "I just thought you'd like to know a tree hit your power line, blew out your transformer, and it's on fire." Disoriented and confused, I replied, "Thanks." We called the police and fire department, and soon enough everything was under control. Why Bubba was strollin' around at midnight, I'll never know. My heart was still pounding at a slightly higher-than-normal level, but knowing that the properly equipped people were handling the situation put my fears to rest.

How often do we shy away from situations or opportunities due to fear? I believe there is such a thing as healthy fear, but in general, fear is one of Satan's primary tools from keeping us from greatness. When paralysis occurs due to fear, one is faced with two options: avoidance or attack. I have struggled with a speech impediment since early childhood; fear is my greatest adversary. Although most people are unaware of my impediment, it still serves as the source of 95 percent of my fear: fear of being exposed, fear of being less than perfect, fear of being second-best, fear of being labeled a "stutterer"; all of these fears have crushed my spirit at one time or another. On the other hand, I have also found if I avoid a challenging speaking situation altogether, a piece of me also dies; I feel as though I am not who God created me to be, and I deliberately choose to take the Lord off His throne, saying, "I do not trust for You to deliver me through this situation." I still use avoidance on occasion, but generally speaking, I daily place myself in challenging situations. Over time, confidence in those situations rises, minimizing fear. As a result, I am more dependent on the Lord; all the glory and honor are ascribed to Him.

Throughout Scripture there are countless examples of noteworthy biblical figures who are paralyzed by fear at one time or another. In Jeremiah 1:6-10, the Lord beckons the young prophet Jeremiah to do His bidding, but Jeremiah replies:

"Ah, Sovereign Lord," I said, "I do not know how to speak; I am only a child." But the Lord said to me, "Do not say, 'I am only a child.' You must go to everyone I send you to and say whatever I command you. Do not be afraid of them, for I am with you and will rescue you," declares the Lord. Then the Lord reached out his hand and touched my mouth and said to me, "Now, I have put my words in your mouth. See, today I appoint you over nations and kingdoms to uproot and tear down, to destroy and overthrow, to build and to plant."

The real question surrounding fear is: Are you able to trust those in authority over you? In the case of Jeremiah, at first he did not trust the Lord. In my story with the power line, once the fire department arrived, I had no problem sleeping because I trusted the situation was under control. It often depresses me how often I am fearful in situations when over and over Scripture states, "Do not fear."

In John Ortberg's book, *If You Want on Water to Walk on Water, You've Got to Get Out of the Boat*, he offers that the single most common command in the Bible is "fear not." He further illustrates his point by breaking down the story of Peter walking on the water. The story begins in Matthew 14 as Peter jumps out of the boat to join Jesus on the water. At first, Peter's eyes are fixed on Jesus and he walks toward Him, but as soon as he becomes aware of his surroundings and turns his eyes off of Christ, he begins to sink.

Did Peter fail? Well, yes, he took his eyes off Christ, but Ortberg argues there were eleven bigger failures who remained in the boat. Only Peter knew the humiliation of public failure, while simultaneously knowing what it felt like to walk on water, to trust God completely, if only for a moment. The eleven other disciples were safe, secure, and comfortable, but had no comprehension of Peter's initial joy. Failure is a frame of mind. Jonas Salk finally developed a vaccine for polio after two hundred attempts, yet he believed he never failed; rather he found two hundred different ways not to cure polio. Would anyone call him a failure?[1]

Fear will occur in your life, whether you face a frightening situation, consider taking a challenging job, confront a colleague, or simply get that sharp pang in your stomach that makes you pause. Fear is unavoidable. Each time you have a choice: to attack or to avoid. Do you trust that the Lord "plans to prosper you and not to harm you, plans to give you hope and a future" (Jer. 29:11)? Much like Peter, if you fall down, Christ will be there to pick you up. If you choose to avoid the fearful situation, you will potentially live with a mountain of regret. Numerous times, I debated whether or not to run for a certain position because I had no desire to make a speech on my behalf. I am so glad I chose to attack fear even though at times I have fallen completely on my face. One of my life mottos has always been "no regrets." In my senior yearbook, my sister placed a quotation underneath my picture; it said, "Live your life as an exclamation, not an explanation." Don't look back on your life and ask, "Why did I allow fear to dictate my actions?" Against the backdrop of eternity, what does it really matter if you fall on your face every once in a while?

↗ ↙ ↗ ↙ ↗

Seasoned Advice

Matt Herndon, 30, founding pastor of Rooftop Community, St. Louis, Missouri: I struggled with despair. A lot of twenty-year-olds struggle with pride. They're in the prime of their life as they set out on exciting careers taking them to exciting places to meet exciting people. Not me. I didn't spend my twenties struggling with pride, but with despair. I was overwhelmed with the independence of being twentysomething. I was overwhelmed by the responsibilities of being newly married. I was overwhelmed by the challenge of making career decisions. My dad had taught me so much growing up, but not everything. And being twenty seemed to present me with more challenges than I was equipped to handle. Well into my twenties, I wanted nothing but to be a child again, where I didn't have to make those decisions or handle that responsibility. It took a long time to learn that being twenty was sort of a "second childhood" for me, in which I learned to live life under the care of my heavenly Father, outside of the care of my earthly mom and dad. As I started experiencing God's care and started better handling the independence and responsibility of being a grown-up, my despair disappeared.

Points to Ponder

1. Read Matthew 14:22-34.

2. What act of obedience is God calling you to do right now?

3. What paralyzes you?
   What is your biggest fear?

4. Share your fear with a close friend.

---

1. John Ortberg, *If You Want to Walk on Water, You've Got to Get Out of the Boat* (Zondervan, Grand Rapids, MI: 2001) p. 16-28.

WHAT IS SUCCESS IN PRACTICAL TERMS?

How does one find a career? Or, in Christian vernacular, "What is God's will for my life?" What if God calls me to be a missionary in a far-off land away from my family and friends? Os Guinness, in *The Call*, defines "calling" as the "truth that God calls us to Himself so decisively that everything we are, everything we do, and everything we have is invested with a special devotion and dynamism lived out as a response to His summons and service."[1] Does a Christian have to live an impoverished and lonely life to be a success in God's eyes? Is it okay if I want to be the CEO of a large bank? Can I buy the dream house that costs $750,000? Questions such as these are ones that each person must answer individually, but I do want to offer a few thoughts that may be of some practical help.

First of all, it's all relative! Truth is not relative, although so many college professors and psychologists want us to believe it is, but within the truth, God judges us according to our own circumstances. For example, a friend of mine knows a man who is worth well over $1 billion. He still works for a large insurance company that bears his name, but he gives away more than 85 percent of his income. While 85 percent seems like unusual generosity, this man would be the first to tell you that he's not giving sacrificially. Giving away that much of his income does not keep him from owning a nice home or enjoying a nice meal. John Piper in *Desiring God* suggests, "The issue is not how much a person makes. Big industry and big salaries are a fact of our times, and they are not necessarily evil. The evil is in being deceived into thinking a $100,000 salary must be accompanied by a $100,000 lifestyle. God has made us to be conduits of His grace. The danger is in thinking the conduit should be lined with gold. It shouldn't. Copper will do."[2] This man proves Piper's point. He lives very well by anyone's standards.

By contrast, there is a story of a widow in Luke 21:2-4: "And He saw a poor widow putting in two small copper coins. And He said, 'Truly I say to you, this poor widow put in more than all of them [the wealthy]; for they all out of their surplus put into the offering; but she out of her poverty put in all that she had to live on" (NAS). Which person is more generous: the widow or the billionaire? In God's eyes, the widow is more generous. So should the billionaire give more away? Should he give it all away and live in poverty? Frankly, the answer is that this would be virtually impossible. Aside from being irresponsible and giving money to any old organization, this amount would be almost impossible to give away. In the end, each person—from the widow to the billionaire to you and me—will be judged not against each other but against our own circumstances. Those with money need not shy away from it in guilt, but they must recognize that "to whom much is given, much is demanded" (Luke 12:48). Those without money should not live in the belief that if only they had more money, they'd be fulfilled. As Christians, we must have a different perspective on everything, including true success.

Some of you reading this will inherit a lot of money; some of you will make a lot of money in your career; some of you will struggle to have enough money throughout your life. Regardless of which category you fall into, the important thing is to realize that God does not measure success by your bank account, be it big or small. He measures success by your reliance on Him. If money is making you self-reliant, you may want to get rid of it.

The key is to live below your means—not in need or in want. Too often as individuals' salaries increase, so does their modicum of lifestyle. It is not easy when your friends are living a certain lifestyle, and you are diligently tithing, or maybe your friends are devoted Christians, but they just make a lot more money than you do. God is your standard, not your peers. God calls each of us to a certain level of lifestyle. As God said in *Bruce Almighty*, some of the happiest people are those who work with their hands. Think back in your life; it's true. My high school custodian and my church's custodian in Winston-Salem both spread joy into everyone's lives by the manner in which they approached their vocation. Each of them loved the Lord and truly lived Colossians 3:23: "Whatever you do, work at it with all of your heart, as working for the Lord, not for men."

As you pursue a career, put aside the money issue if you can. There are countless stories of miserable men and women with tons of money. "'Take it from me,' said Madonna, 44. 'I went down the road of be all you can be, realize your dreams, and I'm telling you that fame and fortune are not what they're cracked up to be. We live in a society that seems to value only physical things, only ephemeral things. People will do anything to get on these reality shows and talent contests on TV. We're obsessed.'"[3] And there are countless stories of miserable men and women with no money, who think money will take away their misery. And then there are a few other stories, stories about men and women at both ends of the financial spectrum who are at peace because they know where real treasure lies; they are not dependent on their bank account to provide happiness. Their treasure is in heaven.

Money is the easy and obvious thing to talk about, as so many people spend their lives in its trap. But people pursue careers for all sorts of other wrong reasons, too: power, fame, prestige, parental approval, peer acceptance, and on and on. My challenge to you has little to do with money or any of these other things. Choose a job for the right reasons; define success as storing up treasures in heaven. If that's the success you desire, you will choose the right career!

↗ ↙ ↗ ↙ ↗

Seasoned Advice

Amy Hartman, 46, director of Falls Church Fellows Program, Falls Church, Virginia: Many Christians think that by following Christ, their path will be smooth and difficulties minimized. I think this age group [twentysomethings] really struggles with the concept of pain and suffering (through lost relationships/ loves/jobs, etc.) and the role it plays in spiritual development. Most of this age group doesn't understand the concept of waiting. I don't mean the sexual context here, but more so, "I want things now in my prescription." With the technology culture and everything so instant (cell phones, instant messaging, etc.), the whole concept of waiting and God's timing becomes less relevant; it seems "so old-fashioned." I see this, too, in the whole job scene where young believers are passionate about their "callings" and not wanting to get bored with work. Always looking for "that perfect job" and then being disappointed when they don't find it. Shift your thinking. Stop looking for an exciting job; rather bring excitement to the job!

John Hunter, 57, retired chairman of the board and CEO of Solutia Inc., Bonita Springs, Florida: As a person enters that time of "twentysomething," it is easy to be unaware of what you do not know, to be overly impressed with what you do know, and to actually believe that you are completely "in charge." Often this is a time of, among other things, graduating, acquiring the first job, selecting a mate, setting off on a chosen career, and starting a family. All your "own" choices and the fruits of your "own" efforts: these are the lures of successes past and future promise that can obscure the reality of your need for God in your lives and the comfort of His sovereignty. And then you are either lost, perhaps not yet realizing it, or there is an uneasy awareness that there is something lacking, something not quite included in each successive accomplishment. You have become the prodigal.

And you will find as you wrestle with this gnawing uncertainty, that the answer is to turn back to God, to return to the Father, whom you will always find waiting patiently for you with open arms. You discover that there is a natural order that is essential to personal success and peace, and that it begins with God and a continuing relationship with Him through Jesus. Unless the spiritual life is attended to, vigorously and with intent, the career, the family, the personal success will fall far short of the blessing intended by God.

I was a prodigal during this time, in my early "twentysomething," although I grew up in a Christian home with strong instruction about and acknowledgement of God. Oh, I did not "demand my inheritance" and march willfully away. No, I was lured away, success by success, in small easy steps ... no devotional today because I must get to work early, skipping church this Sunday is okay ... but I became the prodigal, nonetheless. Fortunately I came to my senses, largely because of the persistence of my wife and upon the birth of our first child. And with my return, God has blessed us in proportion to our faithfulness.

So what I know now that I wish I had known then is how tempting the world can be and how easy it is to be drawn away from the purpose of our creation ... to be a faithful child. So my advice is to keep your spiritual life healthy through an intentional, active relationship with God, and all other parts of your life will be more than they otherwise could be. Stay with the Father and delight in all that He wishes to provide for you. Practically, make a habit of daily personal devotions, be involved in a healthy church, and participate in a small accountability group with other believers. For, by the way, the same temptations and the same easy path to wander away from the estate will present themselves to you in your thirty, forty and fiftysomethings, and while not there yet, I am confident they await me in the sixties and beyond, so be vigilant.

Points to Ponder

1. Write down a list of careers that interest you. Now write your reasons for wanting each career. Do any stand out as bad reasons or good reasons?

2. Begin praying daily that God will give you a vision for your life, one that honors Him above any earthly treasure.

3. List three tangible ways you can bring excitement to your current job.

1. Os Guinness, *The Call* (Word Publishing, Nashville, TN: 1998) p. 4.
2. John Piper, *Desiring God* (Multnomah Books, Sisters, Ore.: 1996) p. 172-173.
3. Edna Gunderson, "Madonna's Epiphany: The Material Girl concludes after 20 years that, yes, it's all an illusion" *USA TODAY* April 18, 2003, Life Section 11D.

WHO'S YOUR
BARNABAS?

Barnabas encouraged Paul unconditionally; he was not looking for fame, glory, or adoration. Instead, he ran alongside someone in whom he believed. In college, a group of us got together to meet weekly with an older, wiser man for Bible study, accountability, and fellowship. Our theme verse was Proverbs 27:17, "As iron sharpens iron, so one man sharpens another." We understood that in order for consistent growth to occur, we needed others to sharpen us weekly. We are meant to be in a community of people, so that "we may spur one another on toward love and good deeds. Let us not give up meeting together, as some are in the habit of doing, but let us encourage one another—and all the more as you see the Day approaching" (Heb. 10:24-25).

Throughout the Bible, there are countless examples of men

running alongside each other for the sake of the Gospel; two prominent examples come to mind: Jonathan and David, and Aaron and Moses. Whenever I read 1 Samuel 18-20, I am continually amazed at Jonathan's selfless actions toward David.

Jonathan is the rightful heir to Saul's kingdom, and yet "Jonathan became one in spirit with David and loved him as himself" (1 Sam. 18:1). As David's prominence grew and Saul's dementia increased, Saul "told his son Jonathan and all the attendants to kill David. But Jonathan was very fond of David and warned him" (1 Sam. 19:1). Time after time, Jonathan sides with David and confronts his father on David's behalf. In the end, "David got up from the south side of the stone and bowed down before Jonathan three times, with his face to the ground. Then they kissed each other and wept together—but David wept the most. Jonathan said to David, 'Go in peace, for we have sworn friendship with each other in the name of the Lord' … then David left, and Jonathan went back to the town" (1 Sam. 20:41-42). Jonathan had every right to resent David, and yet there is no evidence of the sort. He saw David as a brother in Christ, whom he loved. As a result, David lived and became one of the most prominent kings in biblical history.

Another man who successfully ran alongside another was Moses' brother, Aaron. Moses always intrigues me for a variety of reasons, but one rests in the idea that he is always pegged as a man of great faith:

"By faith Moses, when he had grown up, refused to be known as the son of Pharoah's daughter. He chose to be mistreated along with the people of God rather than to enjoy the pleasures of sin for a short time. He regarded disgrace for the sake of Christ as of greater value than the treasures of Egypt, because he was looking ahead to his reward. By faith he left Egypt not fearing the king's anger; he persevered because he saw him who is invisible. By faith he kept the Passover and the sprinkling of blood, so that the destroyer of the firstborn would not touch the firstborn of Israel. By faith the people passed through the Red Sea as on dry land" (Heb. 11:24-29).

Yet, when God first called Moses, he was filled with great doubt in his own ability: "What if they do not believe me or listen to me and say, 'The Lord did not appear to you'?" (Exod. 4:1). God proceeded to give Moses the benefit of signs: Moses watched his staff turn into a snake, his own hand turned leprous and then back again, and God's decree that he could turn the Nile into a river of blood. Even after these miraculous signs, Moses still provided God with another excuse: "O Lord, I have never been eloquent, neither in the past nor since you have spoken to your servant. I am slow of speech and tongue" (Exod. 4:10). Moses continued to plead with God to send someone else, until the Lord's anger burned and finally volunteered Moses' brother Aaron, since "he can speak well" (Exod. 4:14). Aaron served as Moses' mouthpiece to the elders and Israelites. It is imperative to find men or women to spur you along in your faith. A primary way to spur each other on is in the arena of accountability.

Finding an accountability partner is difficult for two reasons. First, it can be tough to honestly admit your struggles. Second, it is hard to find someone who will commit to keeping you accountable. It can be embarrassing to reveal your deep, dark secrets to a friend, especially the first time. "He'll think I'm gross/stupid/unChristian …" we think, and the fear of a friend mocking you or looking upon you with disdain keeps us from taking that difficult step of admitting our weaknesses. But while most people act like they have it all together, everyone is struggling with sins and weaknesses of their own, even Moses. And even if they do not share the same difficulties, virtually all of your peers will be able to relate to your temptations at some level. I urge you to find a friend who you can trust and talk to about areas you are trying to overcome.

What you'll find once you admit a weakness is that the sin suddenly has less power over you. Keeping things secret causes them to grow and to fester like infected wounds, bringing ever more pain until the wound is treated. Sin is a spiritual wound, and it will grow until you take some action to heal it. One of the first actions is to find an accountability partner. It isn't a magic trick, though. There must be a genuine effort and desire on your part to change. In my experiences with accountability, one danger is that you begin to feel okay about your sin because someone else struggles with the same thing. In that regard, it can be best to have a partner who is willing to admit his own, different struggles for which you can hold him accountable. The fact remains that most of us struggle with the same things; males primary struggle with lust (masturbation, pornography), pride, ego, and power, while women generally struggle with appearance, security, and peer's approval. When you find that your friends struggle in the same way, ask God to help you keep from using that knowledge to justify your sin. Pray instead for a genuine attitude of repentance and a desire to demonstrate that you can indeed live by a higher standard. There are two attitudes you can take upon finding out that you are not alone: first, you can think, "Hey, it must be no big deal." Or, you can think, "By striving against sin, I can not only help myself but also my accountability partner to hold a higher standard!" I encourage the latter attitude, as it is the only way accountability will work.

In my lifetime, I have been blessed with many men who have run alongside of me from time to time, but two men have left an indelible mark on my faith journey: my college roommate, Huck, and my college friend, Tim. My college roommate and I lived together for three years, including a semester in Vienna. Needless to say, we have shared countless stories together, including the time when we awoke to find water gushing into our room after a water pipe burst. I still see Huck dancing around giggling while I was shoving everything in sight underneath our door. Huck was his last name, but it was fitting. Huck first introduced me to Christian literature, Scripture memorization, listening to sermons, fasting, writing encouraging notes, enjoying the Sabbath, and creating crazy answering machine messages. Tim taught me vulnerability, dependability, the importance of journaling, asking questions of others, and pursuing people. Both men continue to serve as my Barnabas.

ア ㇰ ア ㇰ ア

Seasoned Advice

Margaret Feinberg (*www.margaretfeinberg.com*), 30, author of *Twentysomething: Surviving & Thriving in the Real World*, Sitka, Alaska: If there was one thing that I wish someone would have told me in my early twenties, it's that you're not alone in what you're experiencing. After graduating from college, I entered the workplace and found myself struggling with the constraints of a 9-to-5 job. I felt like my life was shriveling inside a cubicle. I didn't understand the office politics. I couldn't believe the glass ceiling was so low. And I knew there was no way—on my current income—that I was ever going to be able to buy a home. I was surrounded by older coworkers, people who seemed to have it all together, and I felt very alone in the struggle.

It wasn't until I began connecting with other twentysomethings that I discovered the transition into the real world is almost always bumpy. Once I got past the initial "everything is fine" answers, I learned that almost everyone I knew who was my age was struggling with the same basic issues. The transition from carefree college days to a corporate environment is tough.

But after a year or two, I finally felt like I was in the swing of things. A roof over my head. A small savings account. A used car I could call my own. Then, the deeper questions began emerging: Who am I? What's my purpose? and What the heck am I supposed to do with my life?

That's when I began wrestling with core issues of identity, purpose, calling, career, and passion. What's funny is that those same friends who were wrestling with their real world jobs were now dealing with the same issues I was facing. Together, we were able to both challenge and encourage each other. While no one seemed to have any real answers, there was an incredible amount of comfort and healing in knowing that we weren't alone.

I think that finding authentic community is essential for twentysomethings. We all need friends, true friends. You can't make a true friend overnight, but if you're persistent, the weeks and months will roll into years, and real relationship will develop. I've had several "tribes" or groups of friends, and they've all helped me grow as an individual—discovering my hopes, dreams, strengths, and weaknesses. It's in these groups that I've grown the most—both as a person and as a follower of Jesus.

Points to Ponder

1. Read 1 Corinthians 10:13.

2. List the things that you are embarrassed to tell anyone about.

3. Who are some people (or one person) to whom you tell your "secrets"?

4. Read Ecclesiastes 4:9-10. What does this verse have to do with accountability?

WHAT'S YOUR THORN?

Each of us is multifaceted, with many gifts, talents, hopes, fears, and struggles. We are wired up for reasons we do not always understand and are faced with the reality that we have a choice in dealing with the daily struggles of life: to avoid or to attack. In some cases, these daily struggles prove incessant and relentless, such as the case with Paul's "thorn" in 2 Corinthians 12. Rick Warren in *The Purpose-Driven Life* suggests that "a weakness, or 'thorn' as Paul called it, is not a sin or vice or a character defect that you can change, such as overeating or impatience. A weakness is any limitation that you inherited or have no power to change. It may be a physical limitation, like a handicap, a chronic illness, naturally low energy, or a disability. It may be an emotional limitation, such as a trauma scar, a hurtful memory, a personality quirk, or a hereditary disposition. Or it may be a talent or intellectual limitation."[1]

In the beginning of chapter 12, Paul discusses how the Lord had revealed to him numerous things, but to keep him "from becoming conceited because of these surpassingly great revelations, there was given me a thorn in my flesh, a messenger of Satan, to torment me" (2 Cor. 12:7). Like so many of us who face a recurring affliction, Paul pleaded three times with the Lord to remove his thorn, but He said to Paul, "My grace is sufficient for you, for my power is made perfect in weakness" (2 Cor. 12:9). Scripture does not allow us to know the cause of Paul's thorn. There are many scholarly theories, but in God's wisdom, He kept Paul's thorn hidden from us so that we all could more easily relate.

In the Lord's sufficiency, He led Paul to a place where he could say, "Therefore I will boast all the more gladly about my weaknesses, so that Christ's power may rest on me. That is why, for Christ's sake, I delight in weaknesses, in insults, in hardships, in persecutions, in difficulties. For when I am weak, then I am strong" (2 Cor. 12:9-10). Often, when faced with some severe challenge, we question whether or not we are of use to God anymore, but it is only in our weakness that the Lord may be truly glorified. Countless examples come to mind—for instance, Lisa Beamer, who lost her husband in the horror of September 11, in his efforts to save others. During many interviews and speaking engagements, it was abundantly clear that her hope came from Christ. Or Joni Eareckson Tada, whose ministry, Joni and Friends, emerged twelve years after a diving accident in 1967 left her a quadriplegic. Now, she is a champion for those with disabilities. In their weaknesses, He is strong. As difficult as it is to comprehend "if we have physical or mental disabilities or impairments, it is because God in His wisdom and love created us that way. We may not understand why God chose to do that, but that is where our trusting Him has to begin."[2]

In Exodus, we learn Moses had some difficulty in speech, which is why he wanted his brother Aaron speak for him. The Lord responded, "Who gave man his mouth? Who makes him deaf or mute? Who gives him sight or makes him blind? Is it not I, the Lord?" (Exod. 4:11). My spirit has always been closely aligned with Moses because my speech also has been my thorn throughout my life; I am a stutterer. Over the years, I have spent countless hours of time, energy, and emotion to conceal this impediment. Imagine not being able to say your name or to answer simple questions when ordering. Unfortunately, therapists do not really know what causes stuttering and thus are only able to offer techniques to help one manage the affliction. My stutter emerges as a series of vocal hesitations. In other words, it is a point where my vocal folds lock together, deterring airflow, and as a result, blocking phonation. Certain words, by nature, are much more difficult to say, but fortunately I have been blessed with a mind that sees most challenges ahead of time and can circumvent the majority of these stops, but avoidance is never the answer. Through my "thorn," I have learned to trust more readily in the Lord. Much like Paul, I have arrived at a place where I understand the need for my infirmity. Had I not been afflicted all these years, my character would have missed a wonderful refinement opportunity. As a result of my thorn, I am more sensitive to those who suffer from debilitating struggles. As a result of my thorn, all glory and honor for my speaking successes go to the Lord. As a result of my thorn, I have learned to run with God, not ahead of Him because "God often attaches a major weakness to a major strength to keep our egos in check. A limitation can act as a governor to keep us from going too fast and running ahead of God."[3]

↗ ↙ ↗ ↙ ↗

Seasoned Advice

Zach Young, 53, headmaster of Wesleyan School, Norcross, Georgia, email December 2, 2002: The importance of the Commandments cannot be overstated, but life can be so painful despite all our best efforts to honor God and others in our lives. Many of us have experienced tremendous sadness recently, and it is important that we try to be sources of comfort to one other. Often the sadness and concerns that we know about with our students, colleagues, family, and friends are actually more than we can know. May we be gentle and loving as we go about our daily interactions, especially during this Christmas season, always keeping in mind that more may be there than we realize. May the love of Christ (and the hope that is in us because of Him) shine through each of us.

Points to Ponder

1. Read 2 Corinthians 12.

2. Identify your thorn.
   If you have to think long about it, then you might not have one. If you do have one, write down all of the benefits from your thorn despite all of the discomfort it causes you.
   What have you learned about yourself?
   How does your thorn affect your relationship with God?

3. Share your thorn with someone from whom you've been hiding it.

1. Rick Warren, *The Purpose-Driven Life* (Zondervan, Grand Rapids, MI: 2002) p. 273.
2. Jerry Bridges, *Trusting God* (NavPress, Colorado Springs, CO: 1988) p. 163.
3. Rick Warren, *The Purpose-Driven Life* (Zondervan, Grand Rapids, MI: 2002) p. 274.

DO YOU BELIEVE IN GOD'S SOVEREIGNTY?

There but for the grace of God go I.
How without compassion, can I pass them by?
Oh it could be you, it could be me, the world has cast aside,
But there but for the grace of God go I.
—Paul Overstreet

↗ ↙ ↗ ↙ ↗

Little Darius' tears rolled down his cheek as our bus ministry stopped in front of his house to let him off the bus; he had no desire to leave his little oasis of tranquility. On the bus he experienced God's unconditional love through our students, while his home represented turmoil, chaos, and hopelessness. Darius was like so many Apache children, growing up in a culture where 60 percent of adults were unemployed, while thousands of others were thrown in jail—mainly for drug and alcohol abuse. In addition, his older peers were often tossed in jail for missing curfew, cutting class, or even attempting to commit suicide. Many of the Apache children's first comments to us were simply "pray for my father, brother, mother, or sister who is in jail." When Darius first started coming on the bus ministry, he barely spoke, now his tears spoke volumes.

The bus ministry is led by a man named Pete, who left his job with an automobile company six years ago to love on kids daily. The throngs of kids who run after the bus—which includes a basketball goal on the back, fifty pairs of roller blades, sidewalk chalk, beads, Play-Doh, puzzles, nail polish, and volunteers who love Jesus—evidence Pete's love. Eventually, little Darius was swept up by an older volunteer, Ryan, who carried him to his mother. Our guide told us later that, about a year ago, the bus stopped to drop Darius off only to find a cadre of police cars, blood everywhere, and his older brother shot. During this mission trip, the aforementioned lyrics played in my mind continuously. All the while, I was also reading *Trusting God* by Jerry Bridges, which addresses the sovereignty of God: "He does whatever pleases Him and determines whether we can do what we have planned. This is the essence of God's sovereignty; His absolute independence to do as He pleases and His absolute control over the actions of all His creatures. No creature, person, or empire can either thwart His will or act outside the bounds of His will … If there is a single event in all of the universe that can occur outside of God's sovereign control, then we cannot trust Him."[1]

For those of us in our twenties, trusting the Lord with everything proves challenging. In our ego-driven society it is difficult to understand that we might not actually be in control. As I've grown older and experienced life more, one of the biggest differences between me at twenty-three and now at twenty-nine is the realization that God is truly in control of every aspect of my life; so simplistic, but so true for "there is no wisdom, no insight, no plan that can succeed against the Lord" (Prov. 21:30). In our twenties we face seemingly endless life-altering decisions. Often we wrestle with choices daily and ask, "How do I discern God's will in this or that decision?" I once heard a sermon where the speaker talked about only knowing God's will retrospectively. Meaning, in most situations we will be about 80 percent sure of the right decision, based on prayer, wise counsel, and life experiences. Years later, it is often much easier to look at one's life and see how the pieces fit together.

Bridges also discusses the importance of prayer as a means to align our wills with His as well as express our trust in Him. Understanding God's sovereign will is more than likely an idea we will not be able to grasp this side of eternity. It's difficult to understand why some children have "everything" while others watch their older brother get shot, but ultimately God is in control even if things do not always seem to make sense. Even at twenty-nine though, I am able to look back on my young life and make sense of why certain experiences have occurred. My advice would be to simply relax because "in his heart a man plans his course, but the Lord determines his steps" (Prov. 16:9). Regardless of our endless planning, life will throw us endless curveballs, and ultimately "who can straighten what [God] has made crooked?" (Eccles. 7:13). The Lord desires good things for you. Seek Him first, even when things do not make sense, even when everyone around you appears to be receiving all of their hearts' desires, even when your heartfelt prayers go seemingly unanswered, even when you cry yourself to sleep at night. Our God is good. Every situation is ordained for a purpose. The choice is yours whether you decide to embrace or escape the experience.

↗ ↙ ↗ ↙ ↗

Seasoned Advice

Roberta Martin, 47, pastoral counselor, Bethesda, Maryland: Enjoy traveling light in your twenties. Don't be in a rush to accumulate things that you only have to move and take care of over the years. Focus on building strong, godly, boundary-filled relationships as they are the lasting treasures in life. Be where you are in the moment as that is all you have. Don't miss it by being too focused on the regrets from the past or lingering on the dreams for the future. God has you in the season that you are in because that grows our reliance on Him.

Monte Johnson, 52, financial advisor, Atlanta, Georgia, and former NFL Super Bowl athlete: The three things that I wish I had known in my twenties are:

1. That God loves more than I will ever be able to understand. As a result, there is nothing I can do that will cause God to love me more or less.

2. That nothing happens in my life that first does not get filtered through the hands of God. God is sovereign, and He is in control. As a result, it is up to me to choose to live my life based upon the truth of who God is and put faith in His Word versus the feelings and circumstances that I may be experiencing.

3. God has a plan for my life. As a result, what happens is part of that plan, and it is for my good and God's glory.

Playing major college football at the University of Nebraska during a period when we won two back-to-back National Championships, three consecutive Big 8 Championships (now it is the Big 12) and Orange Bowls was a great experience. However, for me personally, it was a very trying time since I never started during the three years I played at Nebraska. Not having a relationship with God during those years caused me to question my choice to attend Nebraska, my ability as a player, and my sense of fulfillment in feeling that I made a material contribution to our success. That being said, I did not know that all of this was part of God's plan for my life. At the time, I did not know it nor could I see His sovereignty or that this was His love for me. All I could see was the perceived lack of fulfillment. I can remember saying about those years that the only good thing that happened was I met my wife, Phyllis. However, I could not see this as God's love, sovereignty, or plan for my life.

After my senior year at Nebraska, the Oakland Raiders drafted me in the second round. I was the forty-ninth player chosen and, the first ever non-starter in college to be drafted in the top fifty. It was very fulfilling and gratifying to finally be recognized for my contribution. I was drafted in front of All-Americans, the Outland Trophy winner, as well as those who started ahead of me on the depth chart. Again, I did not see this as God's love, sovereignty, or plan for my life.

The first two years of professional football provided everything that the world would define as success. I played on national TV every weekend and had success, money, and satisfaction that I was better than my college coaches recognized. However, I was miserable. I had accomplished all these things, which and according to the world, brings happiness. Even my marriage was strained. I loved Phyllis, but my love was not that of intimacy but of lust. I did not have a clue about the need to nurture, honor, protect, and lead her as the head of my family. I began to struggle with how to handle my success, marriage, and relationships with friends and family.

My biggest challenge was overcoming the notion that all that I had and did would bring fulfillment, satisfaction, and happiness. I began to search for the answer. I ventured down most paths that the world has to offer, and none of them led me to what I was really looking for. What I was searching for was peace. Peace with my creator of whom I did not know was working in my life even before I was born. Then at the perfect time, God revealed Himself as the source of peace I was seeking. He called my name (irresistible grace) September 27, 1975, at 9:35 p.m. in a parking lot in front of a movie theater in Baltimore, Maryland. After saying a very simple sinner's prayer, something happened. Bells did not ring; angels did not sing; but something happened. All of a sudden, the burden was lifted from my shoulders, and God gave me rest.

Points to Ponder

1. Do you believe Proverbs 16:9?

2. What choices do you face today that are challenging?

3. How have you approached these decisions?

4. What is your biggest struggle as a twentysomething?

1. Jerry Bridges, *Trusting God* (NavPress, Colorado Springs, CO: 1988) p. 36.

DO YOU TAKE TIME TO FILL YOUR CUP?

Howard Hendricks says, "You can't minister to people if you are always with them." Lynn Barclay, the director of Young Life for North Carolina, says it another way, "Serve from your saucer, not your cup." Each of us are wired very differently. Some of us are primarily extroverts, while others are labeled introverts. As a production-driven person, there is an inner tension in my life surrounding how much time to spend alone. In general, I have always been an extrovert, but as I have gotten older, there has been a greater desire to spend time alone. As an educator, it is very apparent when I have not spent enough time alone. If I am burned out and tired, it is very hard to have the necessary energy for a caring conversation with the students. Typically, my responses will be curt in order to move on to the next task vying for my attention. Gordon MacDonald encourages us to "make sure that every day is marked with time to give cleanliness and orderliness to your soul. If a man does not live out of his soul, then the world will squeeze him into its mold."[1] Is your life orderly or squeezed?

If I have taken the necessary steps to give order to my soul, I am refreshed, content within myself, and excited to hear what others have to say. Spending time alone is far more than a good suggestion. Jesus desired it enough to get up regularly in the middle of the night to be alone: "Very early in the morning, while it was still dark, Jesus got up, left the house and went off to a solitary place, where he prayed" (Mark 1:35). He could find no other time when it was possible. Another missionary pioneer, Hudson Taylor, found a similar early-morning time worked well for him, 2 a.m. to 4 a.m. It is during such times that you come to understand yourself better, to understand your relationship with God better, and through those understandings to be more capable of knowing and loving other people. How do you feel when you turn out the lights at night? Are you comfortable with yourself, or do you hate the silence? Without knowledge of self and knowledge of God, we are bound to find our identity solely in what others think of us, and that brings disaster. If others define you, you will forever be changing shape until you are just a blob of random traits and habits that were never yours to start with. On the other hand, time alone will transform you into a confident individual whose willingness to stand firm in your convictions will be rooted in a deep, unshakable security through God.

Carving out time to spend with God is imperative; I would also take it one step further and endorse the discipline of solitude. All disciplines have some risk attached, and "in solitude, we confront our soul with its obscure forces and conflicts that escape our attention when we are interacting with others."[2] Many people find it very undesirable to be alone because they must face themselves. They may see insecurity, a longing for the affection of others, or a fear of loneliness. If a person fears solitude due to insecurity, he probably needs it more than anyone, like a boy who refuses to have his cut cleaned because it will hurt too badly. This is the very same boy who is most in need though. If you fear time alone, face it in small doses. You may never love it, but like exercise, it will gradually change you into the person God made you to be. Without it, you will be the unfortunate blob I spoke of a minute ago.

Perhaps you are not afraid to be alone, but you are simply a social creature who finds your energy from being with other people. My former colleague, Adrian would draw a face on the wall just to have company. We do long for companionship and for intimacy, as Tom Hanks showed us in *Castaway*. Much like Adrian, Tom's character painted a face from his own blood on a volleyball, referring to him as Wilson. We need to be in community with people, but solitude is something all of us must face in order to truly know ourselves and recognize our dependence on God. It is rarely possible to reflect on difficult matters when facing constant interaction with people, television, radio, and all the noise around us. For you, time alone may be as difficult and tiresome as interacting with too many people can be for an introvert. But for all types of people, we must not allow our natural tendencies to keep us from a good thing. Spending time alone with our creator and ourselves is good medicine for all of us.

↗ ↙ ↗ ↙ ↗

Seasoned Advice

Ted Haggard, 48, senior pastor of New Life Church and president of National Association of Evangelicals, Colorado Springs, Colorado: Our twenties set the stage for the balance of our lives. When I was in my twenties, I learned that God has established systems of order for us to follow in our homes, businesses, churches, and communities. I wanted to live within His systems, so I determined to marry well, be a consistent blessing to my local church, and be faithful to my friends and those I served in ministry.

Of course, it was not always easy to make good decisions.

There were plenty of distractions, and on my worst days I could not have cared less about God's order. So, I developed a habit of taking three days a month to pray, fast, and listen to large portions of Scripture on tape. This set a template for a practice that continues to this day—once every season (summer, fall, winter, and spring), I take my tent into the Colorado Rockies for three days to fast and pray and immerse myself in the New Testament. This time gives me an opportunity to forgive, heal, rest, think, learn, and orient my life in Him. As a result, I have a context and orientation for the decisions I make in my life concerning marriage, family, career, education, etc. I have the power from Him to do what I ought; I am placed well in life; and I am enjoying each progressive stage.

Life does not have to be as hard as so many have made it. Marriage can be wonderful. Children can be a blessing. Working, earning, and building life's assets can be a competitive game that gives life dimension. With a few basic core convictions that are set during your twenties, your life can be a delight.

Points to Ponder

1. How much time do you spend alone each day? Should you spend more, or is it enough?

2. Why is solitude hard to face sometimes? Does that make it a bad thing?

3. Why do you think Jesus was willing to get up in the middle of the night to be alone? Re-read Mark 1:35.

1. From a letter to author's friend, Tim Blue.
2. Dallas Willard, *The Spirit of the Disciplines* (Harper Collins, NY, NY: 1991) p. 161.

DO YOU LIVE YOUR LIFE IN THE AMBIGUOUS GRAY?

Have you ever "sampled" items from a grocery store? Have you ever shown your old student ID for a discount, even though you are no longer a student? Have you ever been undercharged for something and failed to notify the appropriate person? Have you ever made personal, long-distance phone calls at work? Have you ever charged rent to a roommate and not qualified the rent as income on your taxes? Most of us have dabbled at one time or another in the undeniable gray. Are there really gray areas, or do we cast a shadow of ambiguity in order to appease our troubled souls? "I've got to sample the grapes before I purchase them. Movie prices are ridiculously expensive; they shouldn't charge so much. The service was horrible; he did not deserve any additional money. My boss overworks me and underpays me." Satan always provides an excuse for us. The truth is everything we own is borrowed from God. He entrusts us to be good stewards of His resources. As good stewards, we are to "give to Caesar what is Caesar's, and to God what is God's" (Matt. 22:21). How are we serving God by stealing from others what is rightfully theirs?

A few months ago, a friend and I went to a movie. Ironically enough, a movie theater employee gave my friend his ticket at the student rate. When she tried to do the same for me, I stopped her and told her it was the wrong price. Afterward, my friend was laughing and said he wasn't going to worry about it. I jokingly said, "Is your integrity not worth two dollars?" Max DePree in *Leadership Jazz* says, "Integrity in all things precedes all else. The open demonstration of integrity is essential; followers must be wholeheartedly convinced of their leaders' integrity. For leaders, who live a public life, perceptions become a fact of life. Leaders understand the profound difference between gestures and commitment. It's just impossible to be a closet leader."[1] Christ's transparency drew others to Him. Do your words match your actions?

In Acts 5, there is a compelling story of the early Church's zero tolerance for deceit. God's standard was absolute honesty and rigid integrity from His people:

> Now a man named Ananias, together with his wife Sapphira, also sold a piece of property. With his wife's full knowledge he kept back part of the money for himself, but brought the rest and put it at the apostles' feet. Then Peter said, "Ananias, how is it that Satan has so filled your heart that you have lied to the Holy Spirit and have kept for yourself some of the money you received for the land? Didn't it belong to you before it was sold? And after it was sold, wasn't the money at your disposal? What made you think of doing such a thing? You have not lied to men but to God." When Ananias heard this, he fell down and died. And great fear seized all who heard what had happened. Then the young men came forward, wrapped up his body, and

carried him out and buried him.

About three hours later his wife came in, not knowing what had happened. Peter asked her, "Tell me, is this the price you and Ananias got for the land?"

"Yes," she said, "that is the price."

Peter said to her, "How could you agree to test the Spirit of the Lord? Look! The feet of the men who buried your husband are at the door, and they will carry you out also."

At that moment she fell down at his feet and died. Then the young men came in and, finding her dead, carried her out and buried her beside her husband. Great fear seized the whole church and all who heard about these events.

Those who are Christians know when the Holy Spirit is tugging on their hearts. In this story, this couple misrepresents their piety by offering a partial gift to the Apostles and claiming credit for the full gift.

Are you holding anything back from God? If everything is His to begin with, what does it really matter? I purchased a home a few summers ago. For the first time since earning my own money, I really struggled with my tithe. My tithe has always been a great source of enjoyment to support friends in ministry, but that first year I had fallen into the house trap. More than once I argued, "I simply, don't have the money. I need to get a new water heater, etc." Once I refinanced my house, I made a new commitment to give my tithe first each month.

God's standards are so much higher than anything we could possibly comprehend, but that's why the Holy Spirit is there to help us see clearly. "You have not lied to men but to God" proves a compelling line for me personally. In every encounter, if we truly believe that everything we own is borrowed from God and that we are stewards of His resources, then we should never hold anything back for our personal gain. We are called to follow in His footsteps as people of integrity.

107

Seasoned Advice

Matt Herndon, 30, Founding Pastor of Rooftop Community, St. Louis, Missouri: Have I ever held things back from God? No, not really. Other than, oh, you know … MY LIFE in general. I'll hesitate to share stuff with Him, even though I know He already knows, because I'm afraid of His reaction. I hesitate to confess my sins to Him because I don't want to have to think about His disappointment. I won't give Him control over my life or jurisdiction over my day because of where He might take me, or what He might ask of me. I know this is all so irrational, though. God is love; God is forgiveness; God is acceptance; God is peace; and all that. And I know that I should not be afraid to share anything with Him, or give Him any part of my life, as I know—at least, theologically, I know—that He'll never respond to me in a way that isn't for my ultimate good or for His ultimate glory. But as I am a weak and short-sighted human being, I forget that and struggle on a daily, hourly basis to share what I have with the God who made me.

Points to Ponder

1. Are you holding anything back from God?

2. Do your words match your actions?

3. When do you feel most tempted to give partial gifts to God?

1. Max DePree, *Leadership Jazz* (Doubleday, NY, NY:1992) p. 10.

WHAT DOES A GOOD PURSUIT LOOK LIKE?

On more than one occasion I have been mocked by my peers for seeking new and creative ways to express my heart to a young lady. At times, my actions bordered on the edge of reckless abandon; so much for playing it cool, but I needed to express myself. I imagine my actions might have embarrassed my friends; granted, needle-point, collages, baking, arts and crafts, flowers, and writing songs for a young lady are not typical male activities, but words alone lacked the meaning I was trying to convey. God made me creative for a reason, and "the romantic heart seeks out new and creative ways to reach the one it beats for. People in love do lots of crazy things. Sometimes they even become an embarrassment to those around them."[1] Ladies, for most men, pursuing a young lady proves extremely frightening, even though in our core "there is nothing so inspiring to a man as a beautiful woman. She'll make you charge the castle, slay the giant, leap across the parapets," but "it is fear that keeps a man at home where things are neat and orderly and under his control."[2] Who wants to be rejected? Guys, how often have you heard a woman say she desires to be pursued and feel like a princess? It's our job to step up to the plate, but how? Let's start with the general notion that most twentysomethings are no longer dating just for fun; rather, we date to determine whether this is God's chosen person for us.

Risk: Men should assume all of the risk in a dating relationship. Women should never have to guess where the man stands. Period. Early in our dating relationship with my fiancée, Krista, I told her my intention in dating her was to see whether she was God's woman for me. I wanted to guard her heart, "for it is the wellspring of life" (Prov. 4:23).

Know: Take time to get to know the person you are pursuing. Does this person match up with you well? Does he or she enhance who you are in Christ? Does time away from this person dwindle or kindle? Periodically, it is important to step back from the situation and be objective. Is this the right guy or gal for me? Why? Ask your friends what they think. Spend time with the person in a variety of settings. When dating Krista, it was so amazing to see her many facets as we encountered different situations. For instance, one night while having dinner, she noticed I needed something from the waiter and tracked him down for me without asking. It might seem small, but it was another example of her servant's heart and nurturing demeanor.

Pace: Men need to set the proper pace for dating: "If you find honey, eat just enough—too much of it, and you will vomit" (Prov. 25:16). Dating is a challenging time because even when you want to spend every minute with the person, you are better served to refrain. In addition, the physical aspect of a relationship is very important. On our fourth date, Krista shared with me that she had never kissed anyone. Needless to say, I was a little surprised that this beautiful woman had never kissed anyone, while at the same time, I found myself more attracted to her because she had high standards. As a result, we didn't kiss until I proposed. I respected her enough that I didn't want to take that gift away from her until I was completely committed.

Plan: Take time to plan dates. Most females, regardless of how independent they are, would prefer a man with a plan. Know where you are going, what you are doing, and how you are going to get there. On my first date with Krista, I knew I wanted to spend lots of time just sitting and getting to know her. As a result, I packed chairs and extra fleeces so that we could sit outside on a hill under a canopy of stars and eat ice cream. By nature, Krista is a hyper-planner, but with me, she just relaxes because she knows I'll take care of all the details.

Details: Thinking of all the details shows you care. The day I proposed, I was voracious about preparing every little detail because I knew Krista would notice everything. She did! She sent me a card a few days after I proposed. In it she said, "I love your little details, like lime green roses [her favorite color], bridal magazines now that it's okay for me to read them, dancing, making sure my nails were done before, and the list goes on. I pray I can serve you, love you, and be half as romantic to you as you are to me."

Serve: Serve each other well. Krista and I met while coaching against each other in a summer league swim meet. I drove past her pool every day on the way to mine. Throughout the course of the summer, we continued to out-serve each other with timely gifts. For instance, one morning while my coaching staff and I were putting in the lane lines, Krista arrived with Monkey Bread (a cinnamon bread thingy), juice, cups, plates, an inflatable Gator (our team mascot), and her delightful smile. Of course, I had to respond with an egg casserole and numerous spontaneous tasty treats throughout the rest of the season. Do you naturally desire to serve the other person? Is your longing to make this other person great by helping her achieve her goals?

In closing, allow me to share another excerpt from Krista's letter: "How do you thank the man you love more than any other person on earth for not only making all your dreams come true,

111

but also being more creative and romantic than anything in my wildest dreams! Thank you, thank you for knowing me so well that you knew how to surprise me with what I would love."

Seasoned Advice

Libby Houk, 31, teacher/administrator/coach, Atlanta, Georgia: When I was just out of college in my early twenties, I remember telling my friends that I wanted to be married around the age of twenty-five or twenty-six and have one or two children by my late twenties or early thirties. Even then I recognized the flaw in thinking I could plan the major events of my life such as marriage or children, but it was hard to wait on God and trust in His plan for me when it seemed like the world was speeding ahead with or without me. My lack of trust in God's plan for those areas of my life led to numerous mistakes and regrets.

If I could relive my twenties, knowing what I know today, I would definitely change the way I approached dating, particularly the amount of time I invested in serious relationships with the opposite sex. I was involved in two serious dating relationships in college, and several serious dating relationships after college. Since I considered all of those men possible marriage partners, I felt justified pouring myself into those relationships to discover God's will for me. Ironically, I often became too involved with them emotionally and physically to see clearly God's plan for me, and that hindered the Holy Spirit's guidance of me. Each of the relationships eventually dissolved. When I reflect on those relationships, I remember having serious reservations about some aspect of a man's personality or some facet of our relationship from the very beginning of our time together. Yet I wanted to make the relationship work because the person had some qualities that I truly admired or deeply respected. All of these relationships should have ended more quickly than they did, and some should have never started. If these men had been more upfront in their pursuit of me, we would have moved more quickly to a turning point of drawing us closer together or pulling us apart.

Matt told me on our first date that he would know if he wanted to marry me within a month or two. I was surprised and impressed by his confidence, but I appreciated his clear intentions. I could hardly imagine knowing he was the one that quickly. Yet after dating Matt for only a few months, I believed he was God's partner for me. We spent more than a year getting to know each other, spending time together doing different activities and experiencing life as well as time apart talking with friends and family. This balance helped me to seek God's will for us, and we grew increasingly confident that God brought us together for marriage. Matt proposed to me in September, and we are getting married in June. We will both be thirty-two when we get married; this was not my plan, but it is God's perfect plan.

Points to Ponder

1. Read Ephesians 5:22-33.
   How could this apply to a dating relationship?

2. How would you like to pursue someone or be pursued by someone?

3. What is your greatest fear in a dating relationship?

4. What is your greatest struggle in a dating relationship?

1. Matt Redman, *The Unquenchable Worshipper* (Regal Books, Ventura, CA: 2001) p. 52.
2. John Eldredge, *Wild at Heart* (Thomas Nelson Publishers: Nashville, TN: 2001) p. 15, 5.

HOW DO
YOU DEFINE
SUCCESS?

In recent years, mission statements blazed their way into conference rooms as well as congregations. Groups often get so caught up in crafting their mission statement that they forgot their actual purpose. Overall though, I think setting goals is monumentally important in life. Goals allow you to safeguard those things you deem important. One of the greatest compliments I ever received was from a mentor who said, "Colin, however you define success, you will be successful." His words will forever remain chiseled on my heart. For me, living a life of significance is of the utmost importance. I desire for the Lord to one day say, "Well done, good and faithful servant."

What is success in your eyes? Owning a nice home, having a good family, being a faithful friend, attending church regularly, and obeying the laws are some common definitions of suc-

115

cess. Most of us grow up thinking that Mr. Smith is successful because he has the biggest house in the neighborhood and drives the nicest car, and that Mr. Jones is unsuccessful because he lost his job and got divorced twice. It is totally natural for us to make these judgments, but it is wrong nonetheless. And it is entirely different from how God determines success.

The Gospels are full of God's definitions of success. Jesus says things like "blessed are the poor in spirit" and "blessed are those who have been persecuted for the sake of righteousness" (Matthew 5:3,10). Sayings like these are backwards; they run directly contrary to our standards of success. Success in our world means having things together, being liked, and not being persecuted by people. It means being a generally happy person, not one who is "poor in spirit." Christ's definition of success doesn't mean we need to pursue broken lives and persecution; rather, it means if we live by His ideas of success, these will be the results.

Unfortunately, the world's idea of success bombards us daily. In order to resist the temptations of this world, even the good ones, you have to know your long-term goal: "Do you not know that in a race all the runners run, but only one gets the prize? Run in such a way as to get the prize. Everyone who competes in the games goes into strict training. They do it to get the crown that will not last, but we do it to get a crown that will last forever" (1 Cor. 9:24). Most people give in to pressures because they want to be accepted. They want to be accepted because they want to feel meaningful and significant. In high school and college, though few actually reason it out this way, the person who accepts a beer or drugs is actually making an attempt to find significance. After college, the vehicle changes, but the motive still remains: acceptance. For some it may include choosing a particular vocation because it is "socially" more accepted, while others may merely criticize one's boss in the break room. Either way, the logic is the same; I want to be accepted. Or perhaps the person is more desperate and thinks, "I'll try anything to escape my feelings of emptiness; maybe working incessantly is the answer; maybe drugs or sex is the answer; maybe being a martyr for God is the answer." Regardless of which logic you use, you are trying to fix a long-term problem with a short-run answer. If meaning and significance are what you are after (and they always are, whether you recognize it or not), friendships will never satisfy that longing—especially friends whose acceptance is based on your similarity to them!

Significance ultimately comes from acceptance of whom you are (warts and all) and not from becoming something different. Jerry Bridges writes in *Trusting God*, "In addition to my hearing and vision disabilities, I've never been excited about my physical appearance. But God did not give His own Son handsome features in His human body. Isaiah said of Jesus, "He had no beauty or majesty to attract us to him, nothing in his appearance that we should desire him" (Isaiah 53:2). The portrait of the bearded, handsome Jesus that we usually see has no basis in Scripture. Jesus, at best, was apparently nondescript in His physical appearance, and it never bothered Him nor interfered in any way with His carrying out the will of His Father."[1] People often marvel at the contentment of handicapped people. The reason so many of them are content is that they have realized they can never be something or someone else. Like it or not, they accept the fact that life has dealt them a certain hand, and they learn to live with whatever infirmities that includes. On the other hand, there are some handicapped people who are deeply bitter. The reason for that is simply that they desire more strongly than you can imagine to be someone else. If only I were like Jo or Sally, I'd be as happy as Jo or Sally. Wrong! Happiness, contentment, and joy do not stem from having a new significant other, house, car, or computer. Ask the millions of people who have tried to achieve happiness that way.

A few years ago, I had the privilege of hearing Fil Anderson at a men's retreat. He related many wonderful insights, but one story Fil told illustrates my point well. One afternoon Fil was walking down the beach, lost in contemplative thought. Out of the corner of his eye, a little boy in the water caught his attention. It was hard to miss the boy's bleached blond hair and back bronzed by the sun. As the child turned, Fil could not help but notice that the child had Down Syndrome. Their eyes met, and the boy shrieked with delight, flashed a big toothy smile, and started running toward Fil. Surely this boy mistook Fil for another; what would he do? What should he do? The boy grew closer, and then Fil dropped to his knees, opened his arms, and the boy hugged Fil with his whole being. After a few minutes the boy released his grip, leaned back, then planted a huge kiss on Fil's lips. The mother quickly intervened, apologized, and after a few moments of conversation, they went their separate ways.

Hours passed, and the visual image of this boy remained etched on the back of Fil's mind. What was it? What was God trying to teach Fil from this boy? After much reflection, Fil understood.

The boy's shriek—that's the way God calls us. The boy's smile—that's the way He feels when He sees us. The boy's run toward Fil—that's the way He runs to us. The boy loved him just the way he was … that's how God loves us.

He loves us just the way we are. Happiness comes from the belief that God's design for me was a good one. He wired you with idiosyncrasies that you may not like but also with wonderful qualities that can benefit you and others. Henri Nouwen said, "The question is not: How many people take you seriously? How much are you going to accomplish? Can you show some results? But: Are you in love with Jesus?" The first questions gear toward the world's definition of success, whereas the latter addresses the main point: Are you in love with Jesus?

The long-term goal of your spiritual life (everyone has a spiritual life—it creates the longings for happiness and joy in us) is to find contentment. Contentment can only be found in Christ. Daily, I realize this simple truth. This contentment cannot be achieved by using a short-term fix. If a man has been stabbed, the doctors do not use a Band-Aid to fix his wound. They use stitches knowing that their long-term goal is a healed person. Giving in to the world's idea of success is an attempt to put a Band-Aid over a bullet wound. Recognizing short-term fixes are not the answer can help you resist the pressures that arise. For the Christian, success comes not from the money or power or fame but from brokenness. For it is in brokenness that Jesus begins to mean more to us than ever before. He delights to move into the broken places in our hearts so that He may be our healing: "The Lord is close to the brokenhearted and saves those who are crushed in spirit" (Ps. 34:18). The world's view of success will still seem appealing much of the time, but you must think logically and realize that short-term solutions will only take you one step further from the true answer to contentment: accepting yourself as God made you.

How then should we pursue this type of success? Well, there is no easy answer, no set rule to follow. But this I will guarantee you: No matter what profession you choose, be it a CEO or a carpenter, you will have to constantly fight to maintain a godly definition of success. No matter how pretty your life looks from the outside, you will have to face plenty of loneliness and pain in this life. That's the fact of a fallen world. Where you turn in your moments of pain as well as celebratory moments will determine how successful you are in God's eyes.

↗ ↙ ↗ ↙ ↗

Seasoned Advice

Cindy Sanders, 45, wife, mother, and friend, Atlanta, Georgia: Contentment requires a decision to make the choice to be satisfied with who I am and what I have, rather than to be enslaved to what I lack. And yes, this process changes as we age. Contentment comes from spiritual maturity and the acceptance of the Lord's will for our life rather than our own. I spent the younger years of my life always in a hurry to get to the next phase instead of taking the time to enjoy the stage I was in. We don't need to hurry our lives along, rather let the Lord lead us along. "There is a time for everything, and a season for every activity under heaven" (Eccles. 3:1). If we rush it, we may miss out on God's best for us!

Make sure to spend time with the Lord daily and listen when He speaks to your heart. Be passionate about everything you do and take risks in love. "True" friends are scarce and a real treasure when we find them, so treat them as though a rare and special gift and nurture them to last a lifetime.

Expect adversity, understand that our trials strengthen and grow us, and remember to look for the Lord's blessing as we encounter them along life's path. To achieve those "mountaintop" experiences we must encounter the uphill climb to get there. Take on the philosophy that life is 10 percent what happens to me and 90 percent how I react to it! And know that there is no problem, circumstance, or situation greater than my God!

And yes, there is a lot of truth to Galatians 6:7-10: "We reap what we sow!" I never understood this when my mother shared it with me as I was growing up. The earlier we get this figured out, the better our life will be. I wish I had taken the time to get to know the Lord in my twenties, the way I know Him now. Life is easier when we walk closely with Him. Always look for opportunities to share your faith with those around you. Remember the three Rs: Respect for self, Respect for others, and Responsibility for all your actions. A rich person is not one who has the most, but one who needs the least because of his faith walk with the Lord!

Hugh Sawyer, 52, president of Allied Holdings, Atlanta, Georgia: I was self-reliant and somewhat successful at a rather young age. Therefore, my early successes were likely a barrier in learning to rely on God. The incremental progress that was achieved in my twenties was the direct result of staying active in church and having a loving, caring spouse. By the way, like most people I know … I am still a work in progress. Overcoming ego, pride, and unrelenting ambition served as major challenges during my twenties as well as coping with a rather aggressive results-oriented personality. Essentially, I am highly competitive and like to win … at everything. As a result, learning to submit to God's plan rather than my own was challenging, but necessary in understanding true success.

Points to Ponder

1. What is success in the eyes of your family and friends?

2. What is success in the eyes of God?

3. What is your greatest struggle right now?
   How can you turn it into an opportunity to deepen
   your relationship with Jesus?

4. Where do you feel most content?

1. Jerry Bridges, *Trusting God* (NavPress, Colorado Springs, CO: 1988) p. 162.

ARE YOU A GOOD STEWARD OF THE RESOURCES ENTRUSTED TO YOU?

God equips each of us with a different set of tools. Some of us are from meager means while others are from affluent backgrounds. Some of us have one remarkable talent while others are gifted with plenty. Regardless of your position, God calls us to be good stewards of the resources He has entrusted to us. What does stewardship mean? I define stewardship as our God-honoring usage of the time, talents, and resources God has allowed us to manage. Everything we have is the Lord's. We do not own anything!

For most twentysomethings, time is their greatest resource and their greatest hurdle. If God viewed your calendar or Blackberry, what would He say are your priorities? In the movie *The Lord of the Rings*, Frodo shares with Gandalf that he wishes he had never been given the ring. Gandalf responds that many do not desire their particular situation, but we need to decide "what to do with the time which is given to us." How we use our time is a choice. Human nature drives us toward laziness; Paul offers a solution: "No, I beat my body and make it my slave so that after I have preached to others, I myself will not be disqualified for the prize" (1 Cor. 9:27). Taking control of our time is a challenge with so many vehicles vying for our attention. Log your activities for one week, allotting the appropriate time for each activity. At the conclusion of that week, sit down and calculate your time spent in various activities. Does your log reflect what's really important to you?

The twenties invariably is a decade during which individuals ascertain their greatest strengths and align their lives accordingly. Woven into the fabric of each of us is an imprint of God's design for us. The Lord has blessed me with many talents. One of my greatest fears is the Lord taking away my talents because I am not using His gifts as He desires: "Naked I came from my mother's womb, and naked I will depart. The Lord gave and the Lord has taken away, may the name of the Lord be praised" (Job 1:21). In general, I think this is a healthy fear. The church is designed to arrange a variety of people with a plethora of skill sets. Each person has a role. There is no hierarchy. In *The Lord of the Rings*, the powerful Elvin beauty, Galadriel, tells the ring bearer, Frodo, "This task was appointed to you, and if you do not find a way, no one will." Frodo replies, "I know what I must do; I'm afraid to do it." Galadriel challenges Frodo: "Even the smallest person can change the course of the future." Do you really believe this is possible for you? Do you really believe the Lord has placed you on this earth with your skill set for a reason and a purpose? If you have not done so already, take a spiritual gifts test because "there are different kinds of gifts, but the same Spirit. There are different kinds of service, but the same Lord. There are different kinds of working, but the same God works all of them in all men" (1 Cor. 12:4-6). For most people, these tests confirm our strengths. Align your life accordingly. Bill Hybels, the pastor at one of the nation's largest churches, Willow Creek

Community Church, implemented a team-teaching approach in order to free him up to embrace his stronger gifts. Who are you serving with your talents—God or man?

Do you live your life below your means? Managing God's financial resources well often hinges on the answer to that question. Scripture commands us to "honor the Lord with your wealth, with the first fruits of all your crops" (Prov. 3:9). Throughout Scripture this translates to 10 percent (see Deuteronomy 14:22). In addition, the Bible talks about offerings above and beyond your 10 percent. One only has to look at the abundance of consumer debt in our nation to recognize millions of people are not living below their means. A friend once told me to look at a man's checkbook in order to examine his heart. What would your examination say? There's an old adage that encourages individuals to pay oneself first. The implication is that before you spend money on anything, prepare for your future by investing. I would restate this adage to state: Pay the Lord, pay yourself, and pay your bills. I view tithing as an eternal investment. It's a joy to support friends in ministry and my church and to encourage young missionaries. When paying yourself, remember compound interest is your friend. Over the last ten years, my bank account has grown steadily due to this simple principle. There are many more qualified to speak on finances than I, but I've been automatically deducting funds from my paycheck since college. Not only do you save for the future, but it also lowers your tax obligations. Finally, pay your bills on time and in full. Your credit score is synonymous with your name. Much like your honor, if you screw it up, it takes a long time to earn it back. Whatever you own has the potential to own you.

Simplify your life because "people who want to get rich fall into temptation and a trap and into many foolish and harmful desires that plunge men into ruin and destruction. For the love of money is a root of all kinds of evil. Some people, eager for money, have wandered from the faith and pierced themselves with many griefs. But you, man of God, flee from all this, and pursue righteousness, godliness, faith, love, endurance and gentleness"

(1 Tim. 6:9-11). Honoring God with the resources entrusted to you is a discipline cultivated over time. If God cannot trust you with the small things, He will not trust you with the big things.

↗ ↙ ↗ ↙ ↗

Seasoned Advice

Ron Blue, 61, author, speaker, and president of Christian Financial Professional Network, Atlanta, Georgia: As I look back on my twenties, it is very obvious that the one thing that I wish I had known was how to have a personal relationship with Jesus Christ. I did not commit my life to Him until I was thirty-two, so I spent my twenties mostly involved in a worldly pursuit of success, power, prestige, influence, and money. The reality was that, from a worldly perspective, I was successful, but at the same time I was achieving success, I was losing my family. The Lord in His mercy revealed Himself to me at age thirty-two, and since that time I have both left the business world to pursue full-time ministry, as well as started an organization that was both a ministry and a business. I am now involved in a non-profit organization, teaching and training financial professionals all over the country about how to apply biblical wisdom into their advice and counsel.

What I know today that I didn't know in my twenties regarding finances are five basic transcendent principles of financial success. The first principle and truth is that God owns it all; therefore, I am a steward of everything that He has entrusted to me. The Bible says that naked I came into the world and naked I will leave, and there are no exceptions. Additionally, I shared four things with a congressional sub-committee a number of years ago, when asked what I would advise the American family about their finances. First of all, spend less than you earn and do it for a long time. That is the ultimate key to financial success—living within your income. Unfortunately, we get almost no reinforcement of this at all. Second, I advise people to avoid the use of debt. The Bible says that the borrower becomes a servant of the lender, and there are no exceptions to this. Third, build liquidity into your financial situation; in other words, save for the future, save for the emergencies, save for the unexpected, save for the major purchases, save for the major long-term goals. As you do so, you are prepared for the certainty of uncertainties. Last, have some idea where you are headed; in other words, set long-term goals. When I set long-term goals, such as paying off my home mortgage, accumulating in order to give, providing a college education for my children, starting a business, lifestyle changes, etc., it brings definition to my financial life.

In addition to these five transcendent principles, to me the key to financial freedom is learning how to give. The Lord said in the Sermon on the Mount, "For where your treasure is there will your heart be also." He also said, "You cannot serve God and money." These are two choices that I get to make: who am I going to serve, God or money, and where am I going to place my treasure, in eternity or in this world. Those two choices are very obvious, but they are the challenge that anybody living in today's society must face.

Points to Ponder

1. Read Malachi 3:8-12. How are you robbing God?

2. Check out Ron Blue's *Master Your Money*, which is a good book on this subject.

3. What's important to you? When your mind wanders, where does it gravitate? Your mind's final destination might serve as your greatest challenge in remaining a good steward.

4. It's been said that Christian stewardship is more than the management of things; it is the refusal to let things manage us. What do you let manage you?

DO YOU HAVE A 'WHATEVER IT TAKES' ATTITUDE?

In the professional world, the cards are stacked against you in your twenties. Bill Starling, a college admissions legend, told me a few months before his passing, "Work like a dog the first two years of any new job, prove your worth, then start to decrease your responsibilities to achieve balance in your life. If your employer is not agreeable, then wipe the dust off your feet and move on." My dad said it another way: "Arrive before your boss and leave after your boss." The principles are the same: Display a consistent work ethic in order to achieve your goals. Clear goals are vital. To attain worthwhile goals, one must persevere. Perseverance for me means to be prepared, to be persistent and to be perfect.

129

Preparation is key in achieving one's goals. What are you prepared to sacrifice in order to reach your specified goal? In

Exodus 17 when the Israelites defeated the Amalekites, "Moses said to Joshua, 'Choose some of our men and go out to fight the Amalekites. Tomorrow I will stand on top of the hill with the staff of God in my hands'" (Exod. 17:9). While Joshua fought the Amalekites, "Moses, Aaron and Hur went to the top of the hill. As long as Moses held up his hands, the Israelites were winning, but whenever he lowered his hands, the Amalekites were winning. When Moses' hands grew tired, they took a stone and put it under him and he sat on it. Aaron and Hur held his hands up—one on one side, one on the other—so that his hands remained steady till sunset. So Joshua overcame the Amalekite army with the sword" (Exod. 17:10-13). Moses was prepared to do whatever it took to keep his arms up.

Persistence has always been one of my stronger qualities, for better or for worse. On numerous occasions, I have been denied certain opportunities, but I manage somehow to sneak through the door eventually. I struggle sometimes with the notion of forcing God's will. It's difficult to know where that line falls. In Scripture, Jacob fell in love with Laban's daughter, Rachel. Jacob worked for Laban in exchange for his daughter's hand. After working seven years, "Jacob said to Laban, 'Give me my wife. My time is completed, and I want to lie with her.' So Laban brought together all the people of the place and gave a feast. But when evening came, he took his daughter Leah and gave her to Jacob, and Jacob lay with her. And Laban gave his servant girl Zilpah to his daughter as her maidservant. When morning came, there was Leah! So Jacob said to Laban, 'What is this you have done to me? I served you for Rachel, didn't I? Why have you deceived me?'" (Gen. 29:21-25). Whenever reading this passage, my first thought always is, "How did he not realize with whom he was sleeping?!" Was it really that dark? Some might argue justice is served because Jacob tricked his own father by stealing Esau's birthright. Regardless of the reason, Laban fooled Jacob into marrying both of his daughters and working for another seven years in order to marry Rachel. Persistently, Jacob worked for fourteen years in order to reach his goal. Do you allow setbacks to keep you from your goals?

The Lord calls us to run toward the goals He has set before us. Many of the most "successful" people in the world are not the most talented or brightest, but they run while others rest. Before the Masters in 2004, Phil Mickelson claimed the dubious distinction, "Best player without winning a major."[1] He had received numerous awards through his illustrious career as a tour card holder for fifteen years, yet he had never won a major. After winning the Masters in 2004, Phil Mickelson said, "The harder the struggle is, the greater the reward." Friends, there is nothing sweeter than achieving a goal the Lord has set before you when others said "your goal" was not possible. Be prepared. Be persistent. Be perfect.

↗ ↙ ↗ ↙ ↗

Seasoned Advice

Charlie Fay, 65, retired managing director and former head of investment banking at AG Edwards, Inc., St. Louis, Missouri: I was twenty-three and Edie was twenty when we married. She took my breath away then, and she still does. What I didn't know then was how much she wanted to be a mom. Years went by, and different doctors said we would not have children. I didn't know what to do but pray, not for me (I could accept that fate), but for her. She became increasingly heartsick as all her friends seemed to talk only of their kids. Her sadness, my feeling of helplessness, and my need for God's help motivated my prayer life. After eight and a half years went by, a particularly stressful time led me to decide to spend a night and pray as hard as I could. I was away from home on business staying alone in a hotel, and I was desperate to heal the ache in my wife's heart. I asked God, in the name of His Son Jesus, for a baby for my wife. I asked again as fervently as I could. It was very quiet, and I thought He answered, "Yes." I clung to that thought through the night, bought a stuffed animal for my wife the next morning, flew home, and told her (with only a speck of faith) that we were going to have a baby. Nine months later, our daughter, Julie, was born—a true miracle. Edie's doctor was amazed and felt he had to caution us not to expect this to happen again. He added that if it did happen again, it would definitely be another girl. Five years went by, and my wife wanted a second child. This time, Edie and I prayed together fervently asking, again in the name of Jesus, for another child. Months went by and nothing happened, but strangely I felt we should begin to decorate the room in our home where we would put a baby if we had one. It was a stark room being used for boxes and storage, and we began to fix it up. Well, seven months after our prayer together, but only days after we completed decorating the "baby's" room, Edie became pregnant. Nine months later, miracle number two arrived—a boy named Zachary.

Remember that with God, all things are possible. Choosing schools, jobs, a spouse, a home, a church, etc. can cause crushing anxieties for twentysomethings. Balancing marriage and work, maintaining friendships, and blending families, while keeping your faith in God your top priority, can be a huge challenge. My advice is for you to acknowledge God in all things (Prov. 3:6). Trust Him more, do your best, and worry less. And, whatever you do, do it heartily as if for Him (Col. 3:23). Take the time to talk to Him, but more importantly learn to listen to Him. He has great plans for you beyond anything you could plan, or even imagine.

1. http://sports.yahoo.golfserv.com/gdc/news/article.asp?Source=YAHOO&id=22381, accessed November 11, 2004.

1. Read James 1:2-4.

2. What are your goals?
   How do you plan to achieve those goals?

3. From what setbacks is it most difficult for you to bounce back?

4. Do you believe the "harder the struggle is, the greater the reward?" If so, what actions in your life reflect that premise?

ANY ROOM LEFT IN YOUR MARGINS?

"Break up your unplowed ground; for it is time to seek the Lord, until he comes and showers righteousness on you."
—Hosea 10:12

↗ ↙ ↗ ↙ ↗

In A.W. Tozer's *Paths to Power*, he contends, "There are two kinds of ground: fallow ground, and ground that has been broken up by the plow." The fallow ground lies protected from the shears of the plow "safe and undisturbed, it sprawls lazily in the sunshine, the picture of sleepy contentment. But it is paying a terrible price for its tranquility: Never does it see the miracle of growth." In direct opposition is the cultivated field, the plowed field. The cultivated field has been "upset, turned over, bruised and broken, but its rewards come hard upon its labors ... all over the field the hand of God is at work in the age old and ever renewed service of creation."[1]

These words continue to arouse and awaken my spirit. Drawing the parallel to one's life is easy. A fallow life is one that rests on its laurels, while the plowed life continues to wrestle with life so that it may produce more fruit. Over the past few months, I've been asking myself how my life can produce more fruit. After much prayer and reflection, I came to the conclusion I do too much to do anything well. In addition, I have nothing left to give in my relationships. I've been serving from my cup and not from my saucer and thus have little time to reflect on my life; Socrates' words began to ring true, "The unexamined life is not worth living."[2]

As a result, this year I made a conscious decision to decrease my responsibilities at school so that I could restore my heart through recreation. A friend once told me the purpose of recreation is to "re-create" oneself. For me, recreation includes the creative arts, reading, writing, exercising, watching ABC family movies, and meeting new people. These activities breathe life into my soul. As Christians, sometimes it's difficult to place one's own needs first, but in order to help others we must have something worthwhile to give. Every time I flew somewhere this summer, I was reminded of this concept by the flight attendant who encouraged me to take in the oxygen first and then help the small children around me. Take care of yourself so that you might care for others. In Dr. Mogel's *The Blessing of a Skinned Knee*, she suggests:

> "Winnicott believed that we speed up our lives unin-
> tentionally in order to escape feeling helpless in the face
> of overwhelming problems or inner struggles. This may
> explain why the idea of a whole day of rest is terrifying
> to so many people. We're not afraid of losing time but
> of having time to reflect. Without the usual distractions
> and interference, we may have to confront feelings of

disappointment, loneliness, frustration, panic, helplessness, and exhaustion, and our fear that we are not strong
enough to make the changes we need to make."[3]

Oftentimes, nature intercedes on our behalf and forces us to
slow down, forces us to reflect. A few years ago, I traveled to a
town devastated by an ice storm. Hundreds of thousands were
without power for days while a few lucky homeowners were
spared. I have never seen so many trees split in half as well as
hundred-year-old trees uprooted lying across major intersections.
Natural catastrophes often are tragic, but simultaneously remind
us we are not in control. No power. No TV. No email. We are
forced to communicate and rely on each other for basic needs.
Those who did have power opened their homes to others. Community abounds.

As I was leaving town, a dear friend shared with me her verse
for her Sunday school class that morning, "Then they asked
him, 'What must we do to do the works God requires?' Jesus
answered, 'The work of God is this: to believe in the one he has
sent'" (John 6:28-29). The words struck me as both simplistic and profound instantaneously. His disciples assumed there
was some amount of good deeds they needed to do in order to
receive the food that would forever satisfy their hunger. Instead,
Christ simply says, "Believe." More than ninety times in the book
of John, He says, "Believe." The work that is necessary for all
other works is to "believe in the one He has sent."

Even Christians get caught up in a performance-driven
society. We often feel as though we need to do more in order to
earn our salvation. John Ortberg, the former teaching pastor at
Willow Creek Community Church, struggled with busyness, as
this passage from his book *The Life You've Always Wanted* illustrates, "I was afraid that if I declined opportunities, they would
stop coming, and if opportunities stopped coming, I would be
less important, and if I were less important, that would be terrible. Obviously, then I could cover my schedule with a veneer of
spirituality; I could try to convince myself that it was all about

service—but it was grandiosity all the same. I didn't want to have to admit I have severe limitations. I didn't want to acknowledge my need for things like rest. I didn't want to admit I wasn't Superman."[4]

My new motto is: Life is an adventure to be lived, not to merely maintain. If our lives are so planned, so rigid, we may miss God appointments. My students often chastise me because I am often seen on my computer. Needless to say, a reoccurring priority for me is to stop whatever task I am doing and spend time with those students who enter my office. Admittedly, they often are just bored and want to sleep on my couch, but on numerous occasions when I take the time to slow down, God moves through our conversation. Is your life fallow or plowed?

↗ ↙ ↗ ↙ ↗

Seasoned Advice

Richard A. Swenson, MD, 56, author and award-winning educator, Menomonie, Wisconsin: The entirety of my twenties was spent studying: physics degree, medical degree, residency training program. We all want to be successful, to serve, to live a life of meaning and integrity, to make a difference. So we study hard, we work hard. Yet it doesn't always turn out exactly as planned. If, prior to beginning medical school in 1970, I had written my assumed formula for the perfect life, it would have been straightforward: Great Job + Great Income + Great Patients + Great Colleagues + Great Clinic + Great Hospital + Great Town + Great Church + Great Family + Great Faith = Utopia.

Ten years later, by 1980, I had achieved everything in the formula—except the utopia. Surprisingly, my life was anything but perfect. True, I had a nice house, a comfortable income, a wonderful wife, and compliant children. But something was wrong. I was getting too many headaches, and my wife, Linda, was doing too much crying.

Somehow, unexpectedly, everything had become a burden:

medicine and patients and caring. How could so many good things bring such pain? We were not involved in anything that was bad—nothing unsuccessful, nothing evil, nothing that did not honor God. It was all serving, caring, ministering, doctoring, teaching.

Yet life was out of control. My buoyancy sank. Rest became a theoretical concept. My passion for medical practice and for ministry disappeared. Frankly, I was mystified. No one had taught me about this in medical school or church. If I had achieved everything in the formula for the perfect life, why was it so hard to get out of bed in the morning?

As it turns out, the crying and the headache were both manifestations of the same illness: overload. Linda and I were not only committed: we were overcommitted. We were not only conscientious: we were overly conscientious. We were not only tired; we were exhausted.

What I should have known intuitively, I had neglected to acknowledge: I had limits. I was finite. As it turns out, I am not alone in this. There are only so many details in anyone's life that can be successfully managed. Exceeding this threshold will result in frustration, disorganization, and exhaustion.

How should this concept of limits fit into our theology? As it turns out, we were created this way. We were created with limits. We were created finite. We do not have an inexhaustible source of human energy. We can not keep running on empty. The day does not have more than twenty-four hours. Limits are real, and despite what even the most spiritual stoics among us might think, limits are not even an enemy. Overloading is the enemy.

If overload is the diagnosis, margin is the treatment. Margin is the space between our load and our limit. Margin, as it turns out, was the missing ingredient in our formula. When Linda and I carved out a margin in our schedules, life came alive again.

To defend full-throttle progress and its absence of margin is to presume that all which is good in life and all that God wants us to accomplish is only possible in a booked-up, highly efficient, often exhausted way of life. But His asking us to walk the second mile, to carry others' burdens, to witness to the truth at any opportunity, and to teach our children when we sit, walk, lie, and stand—all presuppose we have margin and that we make it available for His purposes.

Points to Ponder

1. Do my actions reflect my belief in God?

2. Is my busyness disqualifying me from hearing God?

3. When nature presses the pause button are you relieved or frustrated?

1. A.W. Tozer, *Paths to Power* (Christian Publications Inc., Camp Hill, PA) p. 31-32.
2. http://www.quotationspage.com/quote/24198.html, accessed November 19, 2004.
3. Dr. Wendy Mogel, *The Blessing of a Skinned Knee* (Penguin Compass, NY, NY: 2001) p. 221.
4. John Ortberg, *The Life You've Always Wanted* (Zondervan, Grand Rapids, MI: 2002) p.122.

CRAZY
TO WHOM?

Many mornings I awake to music from my roommate's room, probably as payback for my incessant singing during all waking hours (I believe all my former roommates can attest to this). Nonetheless, I love music regardless of when I hear it. One particular song he's been playing lately remains on instant replay in my mind. The chorus of the song, "Spoken For," recorded by Mercy Me, says: "I have not been called to the wisdom of this world, but to a God who's calling out to me. And even though this world may think I'm losing touch with reality, it would be crazy to choose this world over eternity ... call me crazy." Go back and read those words slowly. Now read, "Do not conform any longer to the pattern of this world, but be transformed by the renewing of your mind. Then you will be able to test and approve what God's will is his good, pleasing and perfect will"

141

(Rom. 12:2). Jesus calls us to be different. Jesus calls us to be "crazy" in the world's eyes.

More than a fourth of our student body travels on mission trips during spring break for multiple reasons, but one major reason is to stretch them and push them out of their comfort zones. Year after year, individuals our kids meet seem to make the biggest impact in their lives. This past year on the girls' trip to the Dominican Republic, our girls had an opportunity to interact with a teenage Christian girl, Annabella. One evening, Annabella asked our girls essentially, "What makes a Christian teenager different?" Our girls were speechless. They could not think of how Christians were different. How is your faith impacting your decisions? A dear friend used to say that many parents want their children to have just enough Jesus to make them "good" people, but not to make them different. Jesus calls us to be "crazy" in the world's eyes.

Another friend who recently emailed me returned from overseas mission work. Currently in a place of transition, she wrote: "Almost daily I have chances to witness to people at work. It is so cool when people notice something different about me; I get to tell them WHO that is in my life. It can be so tough at times, but I am loving this time of transition and all the people I am meeting." Jesus calls us to be different and yet a new poll by *U.S. News and World Report* and PBS's *Religion & Ethics NewsWeekly* reveals that "evangelicals—their distinctive faith aside—are acting more and more like the rest of us. They are both being influencing and being influenced by the society around them."[1] Jesus calls us to be "crazy" in the world's eyes.

In John Piper's *Don't Waste Your Life*, he discusses the phrase "wartime lifestyle." He says "there is a war going on in the world between Christ and Satan, truth and falsehood, belief and unbelief."[2] He goes on to discuss how we are human and designed to desire the same pleasures all non-believers crave. After a while, we settle into a lifestyle that is easy and very similar to the rest of the world. The lens through which we view the world needs to be different. We need to continually shake ourselves out of the pluralistic society in which we live. How different are Christians from the rest of the world? How different are the shows or movies you watch from your non-believing friends? How different are you from your neighbor next door? Would people call you crazy? Would Jesus?

↗ ↙ ↗ ↙ ↗

Seasoned Advice

Eddie Staub, 49, founder and director of Eagle Ranch, Chestnut Mountain, Georgia: I feel that my life has been a testimony to what God can do with an average person who is available for His purpose. I've always had a burden for the "underdog," especially hurting children. After teaching high school for two years and a stint at Auburn to get my graduate degree, I went to work at a children's home that was founded by a former All-American football player for Coach Bryant. My desire was to be John Croyle's assistant for as long as he would have me at Big Oak Ranch. God had other ideas.

After working at Big Oak for six months, I started to become restless in my spirit. I began to sense that God wanted me to leave to start a ranch in Georgia. My grumbling to God can best be summed up, "I was a second-string baseball player at Auburn (on a good day) and nobody knows me in Alabama, much less in Georgia; there's got to be somebody more qualified."

But the burdening in my spirit grew deeper and deeper, and finally I knew I had to leave. I've since come to realize that God delights in taking us out of our security so that we have only Him to depend on.

On July 9, 1982, I copied a quote that I believe was penned by D.L. Moody: "Attempt something so great for God that it's doomed to failure unless God be in it," and I packed up my car and headed to Georgia, not knowing anyone. From those humble beginnings, Eagle Ranch has grown to provide a home for more than fifty children at a time in Georgia, and our ministry is currently replicating its mission globally through its Wings Initiative.

Where did all this start? I can point to a solitary night in a chapel in Auburn, Alabama, shortly after my father had died. I was a twenty-year-old sophomore at Auburn, feeling the weight of the world on my shoulders. I was at a crossroads and decided I was either going to live out my agenda or I was going to trust God's agenda. I put my trust in the belief that God's plan was infinitely better than mine. I didn't want to be at the end of my days, look back, and realize that I had settled for second best because I was afraid to go to the "uplands" of God.

Since that time, my journey can best be summed up by a passage from Isaiah: "I will lead the blind by ways they have not known, along unfamiliar paths I will guide them; I will turn the darkness into light before them and make the rough places smooth. These are the things I will do; I will not forsake them" (Isa. 42:16).

Points to Ponder

1. Does your walk with Christ affect your actions?

2. Do others recognize there is something different about you?

3. Have others ever questioned your choices because they were so different from what society might tell you?

1. Jeffrey L. Sheller, "Nearer My God to Thee: Their distinctive faith aside, evangelicals are acting more and more like the rest of us," *U.S. News and World Report*, May 3, 2004, p. 60.
2. John Piper, *Don't Waste Your Life* (Crossway Books, Wheaton, IL: 2003) p. 111.

HOW MUCH DO YOU TRUST GOD?

This past spring, I had the pleasure of driving more than thirteen hundred miles by myself. Most people lament such opportunities, but I relish them. My best thinking occurs in the car. For me, the monotony of the dotted yellow line frees my mind. Thankfully, my headmaster and principal provided me with numerous audio stimulants for my journey, one of which was *The Silver Chair* (the second-to-last installment from *The Chronicles of Narnia*). Regrettably, I have never read the chronicles. Thus, this particular story rang true for the first time.

The young female protagonist, Jill, is given four signs by Aslan, the Christlike figure. He stresses the importance of remembering these signs verbatim. In addition, he requests she recite them every morning and evening in order to increase her ability to recognize them should she come across them. As time proceeds, the

145

adventure begins. At first, Jill's optimism and passion are only rivaled by her zeal for serving Aslan. As the journey unfolds, her selfishness birthed.

Despite encouragement from Puddleglum to stay on the right path, her craving for creature comforts engulfs her and eventually lures her into the Giant's castle. Eventually, Aslan removes the veil from her eyes in a dream and calls her back into obedience. The parallels in this story are almost palpable. In hearing this wonderful tale, the Christian metaphors invade your soul.

If Jill and Eustace had chosen to be obedient to Aslan's instructions, they would have reached their destination much sooner and without as many war wounds. While listening, it was ironic because one minute I found myself criticizing them by saying, "How could they get sidetracked so easily, his instructions were so clear?" while the next second experiencing the "aha" moment of humility; how different am I? How often do I stray outside of God's plan for me due to my selfishness? I imagine I spend more time off the path than on it. This story served as a wonderful reminder … Do I trust God enough to be obedient?

In Scripture it says, "Fear God and keep his commandments, for this is the whole duty of man. For God will bring every deed into judgment, including every hidden thing, whether it is good or evil" (Ecclesiastes12:13-14). E.M. Bounds defines obedience in his book, *The Necessity of Prayer*, when he asks, "What is obedience? It is doing God's will: it is keeping His commandments. How many of the commandments constitute obedience? To keep half of them, and to break the other half—is that real obedience? To keep all the commandments but one—is that obedience? On this point, James the apostle is most explicit: 'Whosoever shall keep the whole law,' he declares, 'and yet offend in one point, he is guilty of all.'"[1] I'm not sure about you, but at times I am paralyzed with fear when I think about *every* single deed I've done or thought about doing coming under judgment. Staying obedient at times can be a monumental task. One of my personal struggles is not to equate my success in the arena of obedience into my perception of myself. Dallas Willard in *The*

Renovation of the Heart explains it better than I could. He says, "We must clearly understand that there is a rigorous consistency in the human self and its actions. This is one of the things we are inclined to deceive ourselves about. If I do evil, I am the kind of person who does evil; if I do good, I am the kind of person who does good (1 John 3:7-10). Actions are not impositions on who we are, but are expressions of who we are. They come out of our heart and the inner realities it supervises and interacts with."[2] At the same time though, we are called to be obedient, even in the small things. I am so thankful to my father for always forcing me to say the mantra, "Anything worth doing is worth doing well."

My students often get frustrated with our dress code. It is difficult for them to understand that in order to be obedient in the large things they must first understand how to be obedient in the small things. Why is it important to tuck in my shirt? In the same way, a young employee might ask, "Does it really matter if I fudge a little on my expense report? I work so many extra hours anyway?" Charles Swindoll says, "If you want to be a person with a large vision, you must cultivate the habit of doing the little things well. That's when God puts iron in your bones! The way you fill out those detailed reports, the way you take care of those daily assignments, the way you complete the tasks of home or dormitory or work or school is just a reflection of whether you personally are learning to 'king it.'...When God develops character, He works on it throughout a lifetime."[3]

Obedience and character are intimately linked. In my short life, I liken obedience to a current in a stream. Over and over I may try to swim upstream or take a break on the shore, but in the end I will get to the point where God desires to take me if I just stay in His stream of obedience. We are sinful creatures. It is so difficult to admit we are not in control. Continually we try to assert control over situations, and painful situations result. A life of obedience does not occur over night; rather, it begins with obeying God in the seemingly inconsequential items. Every day is a test of our obedience to Him.

Seasoned Advice

George Barna, author and director of the Barna Group,

Ventura, California: A quarter of a century ago, I was hard at
work trying to impress the world that it needed me. After college, graduate school, and a wide range of experiences, my real
education refocused my life. Here are three things I learned the
hard way.

First, you cannot lead a truly significant and fulfilling life unless you make decisions on the basis of a biblical worldview. For
more than four decades I made decisions on the basis of my own
best thinking. I worked hard in school, earned advanced degrees,
took on internships and other experiences that broadened my
perspectives, read extensively, and listened carefully to the advice
of pacesetters. I figured that if I approached any decision with
sufficient energy, intelligence, and sincerity, I would arrive at a
pretty decent conclusion.

Sadly, the point that eluded me for so many years was the
importance of seeing the world from God's perspective and
responding to it on the basis of His guiding principles. I failed
to understand that you cannot act like Jesus unless you think like
Jesus. (Read Matt. 16:23, NLT.) Making choices based on my
own best thinking worked on occasion, but more often than not
it left me short of the mark. It was not until a few years ago that
I finally realized the necessity of developing a worldview—that
is, a way of interpreting and responding to reality through a
scriptural filter. It takes time to develop this mindset, and it takes
practice, but operating this way has made an incredible difference in my life.

Second, in my early adult years I was simply too aggressive in
my efforts to make things happen. Eventually, after accepting
Christ and becoming a student of God's words to us, I realized
that I am not in control and simply cannot dictate the outcomes
of my life based on sheer effort and determination. God is in
control and orchestrates the outcomes that advance His king-

dom, regardless of my best plans and most enthusiastic attempts to save the world. My advice to young adults is to relax and enjoy a life devoted to knowing, loving, and serving God. (Check out Luke 10:26-28 and think about what it really means.) Things happen in God's timing, not ours. Focusing on your relationship with Him is more fulfilling and significant than anything you'll ever accomplish in ministry or professionally.

For years I slaved away in vain attempts to get published. Despite experience in government, politics, community action, and academia, and laboring over manuscripts to provide new insights and interesting twists on conventional thinking, every article and book proposal I submitted generated rejection letter after rejection letter. It was not until several years after I put publishing on the back burner that opportunities came to me, without me seeking them, and there has been a steady flow of such opportunities ever since. When God had me in a state of mind where He could use me for His purposes, the doors opened—whether I was actively seeking those opportunities or not.

Third, one of the "big picture" lessons I have gleaned is that many people misdefine success. I know, because I did so for many years. Success is nothing more—and nothing less—than obedience to God. If I live a life that honors and pleases Him, I am a success, regardless of my degrees, salary, reputation, possessions, or achievements. God determines the meaning of success, not the world, because He created the world, He created me, and He is the only one who judges us after we die. Ultimately, it is His plan for my life in this world that gives me value and purpose. Remaining true to His ideals reduces the tension and pressure that I used to feel about such meaningless realities as "getting ahead" or "making a difference." There is nothing wrong with those outcomes, unless they drive my life. God speaks to us in various portions of Scripture about success, ultimately reminding us that all He requires is love and obedience. He does not need me to change the world or to impress anyone else. He made me for His purposes, chief of which are to simply love, worship, enjoy, and serve Him.

We make life too complex. It's a lot simpler than we dare to believe. If you could ask some of our predecessors—Moses, David, and Peter come to mind—I am certain they would echo this sentiment. So, while you're still young and can make the adjustments, get His perspective on life. Relax. Think like Jesus. Live in simple and consistent obedience to His principles and in concert with His purposes for your life. In the end, that's all that matters. You might as well enjoy the journey.

Points to Ponder

1. In what three areas are you most challenged to remain obedient?

2. Which innate characteristics do you find pushing against the idea of obedience?

3. What measures have you taken to help yourself be successful?

1. E.M. Bounds, *The Necessity of Prayer* (Baker Book House, Grand Rapids, MI: 1998) p. 53.
2. Dallas Willard, *The Renovation of the Heart* (NavPress, Colorado Springs, CO: 2002) p. 39.
3. Charles Swindoll, *David, A Man of Passion of Destiny* (Word Publishing, Dallas, TX: 1997) p. 12.

HOW DO YOU HANDLE LONELINESS?

As this year's senior class graduates, a sense of sorrow sweeps my soul. The grass is always greener on the other side they say, but it hurts to see people whom you care about leave your daily routine. In your heart, you know the time is right for them to take the next step in their journey, but selfishly, you ask, "Where does that leave me?" Is my lot in life to encourage others, only to have them depart? You desire to give all the glory to God, but loving others can leave scars. It hurts to give yourself selflessly, yet at times to feel underappreciated or taken for granted, but who are you serving, man or God? Loneliness attacks twenty-somethings: "The yearning to attach and connect, to love and be loved, is the fiercest longing of the soul. Our need for community with people and the God who made us is to the human spirit what food and air and water are to the human body. That need will not go away even in the face of all the weirdness. It marks us from the nursery to the convalescent home."[1]

Do you remember when you first arrived at college? Do you recall the incessant hugging, which freshmen women initi-

ated? I remember a speaker once explained this phenomenon as the need to connect with others. Before tightened security, the airport was often one of the loneliest places for me. Countless times I would walk off the gateway into a sea of welcoming faces, none of which would be for me. I am not alone in this. Many of my single friends, and some married, truly struggle with loneliness. For instance:

> Colin,
>
> Thanks, man. I needed to hear that. It is an everyday thing for me to sink into that tar pit of melancholy. Once I leave the classroom, I quickly reach a low that I cannot escape. Hobbies, working out, reading, etc. get me nowhere. I try to rationalize it, but when it really hits me is when I turn out the lights and stare at the dim shadows of the popcorn ceiling. Even praying makes me wonder if it is just some other means of keeping my mind off the fact that we are alone. I don't know if it is loneliness or just a severe case of boredom with everything.
>
> Nick, 27, Jacksonville, Florida

John Ortberg suggests that although loneliness is common for women, it is "epidemic among men. One survey indicated that 90 percent of the male population in America lack a true friend."[2] Why is loneliness rarely talked about? Why are we so fearful? Has society preached self-reliance and independence so incessantly, that to admit we need others is to claim defeat?

For me, loneliness often attacks the fiercest when I am successful. I know that might sound odd, but when the Lord allows me to be victorious in some endeavor, I want to share it with those closest to me. How many times have I driven alone after a wonderful evening, wishing I had someone to share in the glory of the moment? How many times have I longed for someone to hold my hand when I am hurting? How many times have I longed for someone to tell me a simple, "Everything will be okay?"

If you have ever felt loneliness, you are in good company. Even Jesus felt loneliness. In the Garden of Gethsemane before Judas betrayed Him, Jesus asked His disciples to stay awake with Him numerous times, "My soul is overwhelmed with sorrow to the point of death. Stay here and keep watch with me" (Matt. 26:38). Jesus knew what was about to happen. He desired companionship; He did not want to be alone. Unfortunately, upon returning to His disciples, He found them sleeping: "Could you men not keep watch with me for one hour?" He asked Peter. "Watch and pray so that you will not fall into temptation. The spirit is willing, but the body is weak" (Matt. 26:40-41). Later in Scripture, Jesus felt even lonelier when He lacked communion with God so He could bear the brunt of the world's sins. Imagine spending eternity in communion with the Lord and then when you needed Him the most, He appears to be absent. This is when Christ cried out, "My God, my God, why have you forsaken me?" (Matt. 27:46).

I think the truth of the matter is that this side of eternity we are going to feel loneliness to some degree. Dr. Larry Crabb, in his book *Inside Out*, suggested, "No matter how closely we walk with the Lord, we cannot escape the impact of a disappointing and sometimes evil world. A core sadness that will not go away is evidence not of spiritual immaturity, but of honest living in a sad world ... I'm encouraged when other Christians tell me of their doubts, frustrations, and discouragements. I discover I'm not alone, and I draw hope from others who are learning how God can meet them in their struggles."[3] The best way to combat loneliness is to share your feelings with others. It sounds incredibly simple, but tell your friends what is really going on with you. I imagine men struggle with loneliness slightly more than women, because by nature, we are not as vocal about our hopes, desires, doubts, and fears. Loneliness may attack twentysomethings, but it does not have to prove victorious.

↗ ↙ ↗ ↙ ↗

Seasoned Advice

Susan Yates, 58, speaker and author, Falls Church, Virginia:
I was a student in my twenties, and I was having a rough time in my newfound relationship with Christ. Several months before, I had come to know Christ. I knew my life had been changed, and I desperately wanted to live for Him. I didn't have an exciting testimony. I'd been basically a good kid and had been pretty successful in almost everything I had attempted. But now I felt like I was failing. The harder I tried to live for Christ, the worse I felt. Maintaining pure thoughts, loving others unconditionally, seeking to serve rather than to get, telling others about Him—it was so hard. And in the midst of my confusion, I felt very lonely.

Has anyone else ever felt this way? I wondered. *Perhaps being a Christian doesn't work for me. I can't seem to do it right. I guess I'm just not a good candidate for this depth of commitment.*

I knew my friend who had led me to Christ was praying for me. Even though I didn't feel it was working, I sensed a need to be honest with him and to thank him for what he had tried to do. So I wrote him a letter explaining my frustrations and basically said, thanks anyway. I was very surprised to receive a letter back:

> Susan, I know just how you feel. In fact, most new believers can identify with your struggle. Living the Christian life isn't up to us. It is not try harder. Instead, it's coming to the place where we say, "I can't do this Lord. You will have to do it in me." Then His Holy Spirit takes over and begins to work through us. Walking with Christ is not about you trying to succeed in one more thing. It's about relinquishing. It's about you realizing that you can't do it and letting Him take over.

It's a completely different mindset than you are used to living, and it will take time to learn this. You are not alone. We will all go through similar struggles.

This was a turning point in my newfound journey. Not only did I need to hear his answer, but I learned a valuable lesson. As we grow in our faith, we will experience hard questions that aren't unique to us! Others have gone through similar things. It is important that we not try to "work it out" in isolation but instead seek the counsel of someone who has been a believer longer than we have. We cannot grow alone. God made us for community. It may be that even today you have a need to seek the encouragement of an older believer. Take the initiative. Seek out someone. If the first person you talk with is not helpful, talk with another. God will either provide answers or He will give you a peace about living with your questions. And in the process you will experience the comfort of community.

Points to Ponder

1. Read Matthew 26:36-46. How do you think Jesus felt?

2. When do you feel the loneliest?

3. In whom do you confide?

4. Identify three people with whom to share your feelings about loneliness this week.

1. John Ortberg, *Everybody is Normal Till You Get To Know Them* (Zondervan, Grand Rapids, MI: 2003) p. 18
2. Ibid., p. 29
3. Larry Crabb, *Inside Out* (NavPress, Colorado Springs, CO: 1988) p. 74.

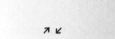

HOW DOES ONE WAIT ON GOD'S TIMING?

For most twentysomethings, life is a series of waiting cycles. We wait to complete college to begin life, then we wait for the perfect job, then we realize the perfect job wasn't so perfect so we wait for God to reveal His path for us, all the while waiting for God to bring the "perfect" mate. If we're blessed with marriage, then we continue to re-evaluate our career direction and often have to wait for God to bless us with children. I have been incredibly surprised by how many of my friends have longed for children, but for one reason or another God shut that door; in most cases, the door was eventually opened either through natural birth or adoption. Throughout this series of waiting cycles occurs an interesting paradigm: How does one wait? In perusing various pieces of Christian literature, there are various perspectives on the subject. Oswald Chambers in *My Utmost*

157

for His Highest suggested: "Never run before God gives you His direction. If you have the slightest doubt, then He is not guiding. Whenever there is doubt—wait."[1] In apparent contradiction, Eugene Peterson in *A Long Obedience in the Same Direction* said: "Waiting does not mean doing nothing. It is not fatalistic resignation. It means going about our assigned tasks, confident that God will provide the meaning and the conclusions. It is not compelled to work away at keeping up appearances with bogus spirituality. It is opposite of desperate and panicky manipulations, of scurrying and worrying."[2]

We all have unfulfilled desires. God's desire for us to wait inevitably drives us closer to Him or further from Him, depending on how each individual responds. As you can see by the excerpts, it often becomes foggy how we should wait. Scripture is our refuge. Too often I rely on Christian literature for nourishment as opposed to God's love letter to me. Quite frankly, it is easier to read a book than it is to dissect Scripture, but whenever I delve into the Scriptures, God reveals healthy nuggets. His Word is so profound, and at the same time, so simple: "I wait for the Lord, my soul waits, and in his word I put my hope. My soul waits for the Lord more than watchmen wait for the morning, more than watchmen wait for the morning" (Ps. 130:5-6).

This passage is such an applicable passage for a twenty-something. The first portion demonstrates David's deep-seated passion, "I wait for the Lord, my soul waits." David does not just wait for the Lord, but his "soul" waits for the Lord. Our deepest longings reside within our soul. Oftentimes, I feel we do not even know what these longings may be; thus, we need the Holy Spirit to intercede on our behalf. In other words, David is saying, "I will wait on the Lord to give me the deepest longings of my soul AND, most importantly, my hope rests in Scripture." The first part of waiting is to ensure your hope is in Scripture and not in the lies of this world.

The second component of waiting revolves around the second part of this verse. Watchmen stand guard in the night, in the darkness. At times they grow weary, at times they wonder why they perform their duties, but in the end, they trust another day will come, another sun will rise. Watchmen perform the duties God entrusted to them with diligence until the sun rises, or until enlightenment comes. In the same way, we should hope in the promises God gives us in Scripture while continuing to perform the duties God has entrusted to us, "As for God, his way is perfect; the word of the Lord is flawless. He is a shield for all who take refuge in him" (Ps. 18:30). God's timing is inexplicably perfect.

I recently viewed the film, *Bruce Almighty*. For those of you not familiar with the movie, Jim Carrey's character is endowed with God's powers. Soon after receiving the powers, Bruce begins to hear voices in his head, people's prayers. He orders the prayers to be filed in his computer so he can respond to them via email. The prayers continued to grow ... so many needs, so many desires (and this only represented one block of people). Restlessly he responds in a mass email to everyone's prayers: "Yes." He responds, "Now, everyone's happy." That's what we think, isn't it? If God would answer our prayers exactly how we want them, we'd be happy. In the movie, chaos ensues as a result of Bruce's mass email. Waiting drives us closer and makes us more reliant on God. He is the ultimate gift-giver. Growing up in an instantaneous society (instant messaging, cell phones, wireless remotes, etc.) makes waiting more difficult, but God's timing is perfect.

⤢ ⤡ ⤢ ⤡ ⤢

Seasoned Advice

Tara Dawn Christensen, 31, Miss America 1997, speaker, and singer: The decade of the twenties is such an exciting time of life! There were many thrilling moments for me in that time frame, as well as several life-changing decisions. During those years, I graduated with a bachelor's degree and started a master's degree (which I finished at age 30!); persistently pursued the title of Miss America and finally won; met and married my husband; and started a speaking and singing career, which is still my occupation. So many changes —so many decisions! These have certainly been wonderful times, but they can also involve a great deal of stress as we make very important decisions. Most likely, you know people who have solid Christian backgrounds, but who have walked a different direction during their twenties. They are making poor choices, some of which will haunt them forever. How do we confidently approach a time of life that has many unknowns and may alter our lives forever? It is only through Jesus Christ. When faced with temptations seemingly too hard to manage, look to Christ. He is always there, rooting for us to make the right choices, and He promises that He will give us the strength to resist the negative forces (1 Cor. 10:13). What do you do when you are concerned about the outcome of a decision? Look to Christ. He knew the days of our lives before we were born (Ps. 139:16), and we can rest in the peace of knowing He is in control. Stay focused on Jesus through this adventurous, sometimes tumultuous season of life, and He will always be there for you. He is your biggest fan.

Ben Tomlin, 32, screenwriter, Los Angeles, California: Twentysomethings: Don't rush. Any of it. It's the twenty-first century. God willing, if we eat well and exercise, we could live a century. So this is a great time to take the big risks, chance failure, and experience life. Thirtysomethings: Get a job. You're thirty.

TIME

1. http://www.gospelcom.net/rbc/utmost/01/04/, accessed November 18, 2004.
2. Eugene H. Peterson, *A Long Obedience in the Same Direction* (InterVarsity Press, Downers Grove, IL: 1980) p. 139.

Points to Ponder

1. What is a deep longing of your heart that has not been fulfilled?

2. What is most difficult about the waiting period?

3. Can you recall a time, retrospectively, you were glad your timing did not prevail?

↗ ↙

HOW DO I
KNOW IF I'VE
FOUND THE
RIGHT PERSON?

This question rings true for me because I just proposed to a wonderful young lady who has been in my life for the last six months. Throughout my life, I have always desired to settle for nothing less than God's best. In regard to a mate, you must know yourself, know God's model, and know what type of person you long to marry.

I am a thirty-year-old man who is overflowing with gratitude that I waited on the Lord's timing. Not surprisingly, I could not have scripted this relationship any better. Over the years, through friendships, dating relationships, and many roommates, the Lord has offered me a clear picture of my strengths and challenges. Needless to say, I am not the same person as the college kid who washed his sheets twice a year whether they needed it or not. Take a critical inventory of yourself. Ask those closest to

163

you how they see you. What type of person would complement you? For instance, one of my past girlfriends was an incredible writer and encourager. Through that relationship, I understood the necessity of being yoked to a relentless encourager. I am a visionary and a pioneer. At times I will push the envelope and need someone who will spur me on in multiple endeavors. Simultaneously, not all of my ideas are good ones. Thus, I need a woman who is willing to speak frankly with me. People are in your life for a reason. The Lord will teach you lessons until you understand. Take it from me: do your best to learn these lessons the first time around.

In Scripture, the Lord offers a wonderful model of His timeline for a Christian marriage. In Genesis 24, we watch the story of Isaac and Rebekah unfold. Abraham desired his son, Isaac, to wed a woman from his homeland. As a result, his servant traveled in search of a woman. The servant prayed for wisdom and discernment (Gen. 24:12-14), found a beautiful virgin who was busy serving (Gen. 24:16), and then received her parents' approval (Gen. 24:50-51). This is obviously the abridged version, but let's take a moment to look at the steps:

- **Step 1:** Isaac trusted in someone wiser than he, his father, to provide the right woman for him. He understood the importance of resting on the wisdom of others.

- **Step 2:** The seeker prayed for guidance. For many years now, countless friends have been interceding on my behalf.

- **Step 3:** The woman was available. This may seem overly simplistic, but if the guy can never contact you, it makes starting a relationship amazingly more difficult.

- **Step 4:** She was busy with the tasks the Lord set before her. Although she was available, she was not idle. Continue to serve in the capacities the Lord has called you.

- **Step 5:** The parents approved of the union. Regardless of whether or not parents are believers, in most cases, they still know your personality the best. Trust your parents.

God has provided countless models in Scripture to use as our guide. The world's standards should not be our standards.

Finally, create a clear picture of the type of person you desire to marry. After college, a mentor challenged me to write down qualities of my "dream wife." "Our God is a God of details," he would say. Reluctantly, I wrote down this list:

- Passionate about Christ
- Sweet spirit (gentle, nurturing, comforting, caring)
- Wonderful mother (wants kids)
- Great legs, angelic face, sparkling eyes
- Athletic
- Smiles often
- Someone who can spur me on—always by my side encouraging me
- Won't settle for anything but God's best
- Appreciates me and the way that I am wired up
- Will sharpen me—we glorify God better together than we do apart
- Musically gifted—or at least someone who encourages me
- Embraces and encourages my passion for life
- We can serve in ministry together
- Loves me as passionately as I love her
- A good communicator—let's me know what she's feeling
- Demeanor of Lynn—do anything, go anywhere for Christ
- Someone who loves to be held and will allow me to provide, protect, respect, honor, and cherish her
- As little emotional and physical baggage as possible
- Prayer warrior (Summer 1997)

165

I never desired to place God in a box; rather, I wanted to recognize those traits, both physical and emotional, that were important to me. When I met my future wife last summer, I knew during the first date that she was exactly the type of woman with whom I longed to spend the rest of my life: "So Jacob served seven years to get Rachel, but they seemed like only a few days to him because of his love for her" (Genesis 29:20). Scanning this list for the first time in many years, I am overwhelmed by God's amazing providence. I do not deserve a woman this wonderful, and yet the Lord chose to bless me with a woman who exceeds this list. Only God could orchestrate two people meeting at a summer league swim meet. Only God could encourage me to wear her favorite outfit on our first meeting. Only God could lead her to my alma mater to lead Bible studies and disciple young woman. Only God could keep two people apart for just the right amount of time until both people were ready for each other. God's timing is always perfect. Know yourself. Know God's model. Know the type of person you want to marry.

↗ ↙ ↗ ↙ ↗

Seasoned Advice

Dr. Jack Wilkerson, 52, dean of the Wayne Calloway School of Business and Accountancy at Wake Forest University, Winston-Salem, North Carolina: The biggest thing I wish I had taken the time to really know/understand was how to love my wife. Included in this response for me are all aspects of the marital relationship—physical, emotional, etc. I don't view myself as particularly selfish (though I'm certain there is blindness in this), but I've never really taken the time to know my wife well enough to love her really well. I've thought that I'd really like to have the following on my tombstone: "He loved well, and he was loved well." I have been loved well, but I've got a way to go before the first phrase will be true.

Peter Kaszycki, 48, president of ProTech, Atlanta, Georgia: My piece of advice is to not marry someone who you are in love with. Sounds strange but here's my reasoning. You should find a life partner that you first off "like" and then "love." Way too many marriages are based on love only (which, to many translates into sex). This is okay but will lead, eventually, to an unhappy, unfulfilled marriage. Instead, find someone who shares your beliefs and someone who you enjoy being with "as a friend." Yes, you should still love them, but you must like them even more. I've been married to my best friend for twenty-five years, and I have seen many unhappy couples that started out strong only end up weak. And then, if they divorce, the kids pay the ultimate price.

Points to Ponder

1. Read Genesis 24.

2. What are your strengths? Challenges?

3. Ask someone who knows you well to answer question #2.

4. What type of person do you desire to marry?

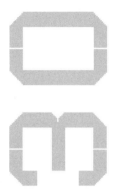

WHAT'S YOUR STORY?

A good friend of mine passed away the summer of 2002. As a preteen, he unlocked my imagination, dared me to dream, and inspired me to hope. His ability to paint pictures through language was amazing. Endless nights I would lie awake awaiting the results of a West Coast game … "Deuces are wild, two men on, two out … There goes Coleman off second, Smith follows suit … the Cardinals are off and running … Tommy Herr laces one down the line, Coleman into score, Ozzie into score … the Cardinals win it, folks. Go crazy!" He would always sign off with "So long for just a while." I never met him, but I knew his voice well. When I heard of Jack Buck's passing, I was alone. Tears began to well up in my eyes as I read countless stories on the web about his impact on the St. Louis community. Mr. Buck was a storyteller. He invited others to see through his eyes, and as a result, millions mourned his loss. I've always been incredibly envious of individuals who can tell great stories. One evening last year I found myself entranced by a colleague's fishing stories. If truth were told, I'm not one who others would call a fisherman … yet, Dick's ability to masterfully tell stories baited me hook, line, and sinker … those are fishing terms from what I hear.

We're all drawn to a good story, aren't we? Have you ever asked yourself why? My mom was a reading specialist for more than thirty years and still consults for Scholastic Book Company. As a result, she gets hundreds of books for my four-year-old niece, Bella. Whenever I visit with Bella, she always wants me to read her story after story. The stories Bella enjoys the most are those she already knows.

Henri Nouwen suggests, "We can dwell in a story, walk around, find our own place. The story confronts but does not oppress; the story inspires but does not manipulate. The story invites us to an encounter, a dialog, a mutual sharing. A story that guides is a story that opens a door and offers space in which to search and boundaries to help us find what we seek …"[1] Stories are important to us because they appeal to the longings of our hearts. Great stories pull at our core, don't they? Yearnings of our hearts are exposed by our reactions to stories. In an interview in *Parade* magazine, actor Harrison Ford said, "Acting is storytelling, and emotionally I'm drawn to stories," which explains after the confusion of September 11, 2001 why movie attendance was up 19 percent in the summer of 2002.[2] People desire a sense of security. They want to know their lives still have a happy ending. Stories are important to us because they appeal to the longings of our hearts.

The first time I met Bill Bufton, our middle school dean of students, the first question he asked me was, "What's your story?" He was trying to get at the heart of who I was … what was important to me, where I have been … in short, my story. Every year, at least once, my colleagues hear the story behind our school, Wesleyan. Our story is one that needs to be firmly entrenched in our minds because it reminds us of our roots and

God's overwhelming hand in forming this place. I am at Wesleyan because I was drawn to its story. I met with Mr. Young, headmaster, one afternoon while I was still working for Wake Forest, and I was sold. I long to be a part of great things, and I am so thankful to have an opportunity to work at an institution that not only allows us, but encourages us to tell the greatest story ever told, about the "perfect" teacher who died so that we may be a part of His story. Is embracing Christ's story your greatest longing?

So many people in their twenties are longing for purpose in their lives. In the summer 2002 I was part of a program for young teachers in private education. Throughout the program, well-known speakers would address us on various issues. One morning a well-known teacher from an Ivy League school spoke to us. From the onset he came in swearing and showing us graphic college T-shirts in hopes of causing an emotional reaction. Much to my surprise, about halfway through his lecture, numerous people around me started to break down; they were sobbing. Here is an excerpt from my journal on that day:

> All around me colleagues lay bare, souls exposed, longing for purpose in their lives. Trapped in a pluralistic, post-modern, relativistic society, how does one determine what is right? By what standards, values, and morals do they live their lives? Each of them overwhelmed by the incessant demands placed on them as educators, yet many of them have no anchor, no well from which to draw the water ... where do they find solace in the dark winter days? My heart mourns because some dear friends are too prideful to believe something greater than themselves controls their destiny.

I emerged from his talk so eternally thankful that I know whom I am, but more importantly, whose I am. In addition my heart overflowed with gratitude that I work at an institution that unabashedly allows me to spread the Gospel. As peer after peer broke down in tears, I realized how so many around me were searching for significance in their lives, searching for meaning. Christ is the only answer. Is embracing Christ's story your greatest longing?

Elise Wiesel said, "God made man because He loves stories."[3] Psalm 139 says, "For you created my inmost being; you knit me together in my mother's womb. I praise you because I am fearfully and wonderfully made; your works are wonderful. I know that full well. My frame was not hidden from you when I was made in the secret place. When I was woven together in the depths of the earth, your eyes saw my unformed body. All the days ordained for me were written in you book before one of them came to be" (Psalm 139:13-16).

We are all here for a reason. We all have our stories to tell and so do those around us. Robert Coles suggests that "people come to us to bring us their stories. They hope ... that we understand the truth of their lives."[4] The challenge is showing others we are all part of a larger story, a better story than the one here on earth. The only way they'll be drawn to Christ's story is if we are able to serve from our saucer ... if our lives are so full of Christ's amazing love that our peers and our colleagues can sip from our excess until they themselves can drink from the water, which never runs dry. Again, is Christ's story your greatest longing?

Stories are important to us because they appeal to the longings of our hearts. The greatest longing of our hearts rests in a relationship with Jesus Christ, whether we acknowledge it or not. Are others more drawn to Christ for having known you? What are the longings of your heart? If Christ's story truly is a longing of your heart, what are you doing about it? How are you deepening your bond with Christ? In the *St. Louis Post-Dispatch* it stated, "Jack Buck, one of America's great storytellers, died Tuesday ... Mr. Buck was often asked to sum up his life. He responded with a little story recalling the day his wife ... asked what he would say to the Lord when they met at the gates of heaven. Responded Jack: "I want to ask Him why he's been so good to me"[5]. God has been so good to all of us. Is embracing

Christ's story the greatest longing of your heart … if so what are you doing about it?

↗ ↙ ↗ ↙ ↗

Seasoned Advice

Barb Bradley Hagerty, 44, Washington correspondent, National Public Radio, Washington, D.C.: There are many flavors of legacy: one's home life, children, friends, ministry, but as I have been single for most of my forty-four years (excepting the last eighteen months of wonderful marriage), I will talk of the legacy I hope my career will leave.

When I was in my twenties, I was ridiculously ambitious. I wanted to win a Pulitzer Prize (then I was a newspaper reporter for *The Christian Science Monitor*). I wanted to do investigative stories for *60 Minutes*. My world revolved around work, and in that sense, my sense of self-worth hinged precariously on transitory things: whether people liked my articles, whether I was given a chance to cover the big stories, whether I was meeting my five-year goals. The irony of making your work your "god" is that it's pretty simple to gain approval from others and a sense of momentum and progress. All you have to do is work harder, and you will surely become better at your craft and be more recognized for your efforts. Things are simple when work rules your life. Now, don't get me wrong: I was not mean or immoral, I did not take shortcuts or stab people in the back. I was just focused.

It wasn't until I was nearly thirty-six that I bumped into Christ in a serious way, that I began to think about life beyond my pen and notepad. I began to think about serving God rather than feeding my career. I felt free for the first time—unfettered by ambition, simply available to pursue the adventure that God had in store for me, wherever that path led.

As it turned out, the path led to NPR a few months after that. But when I came to NPR, I was a very different person. I was there to pursue truth, looking through the lens of Truth, and bringing some discernment and insight to the issues. My goal became—not, did I get this story first?—but, is this story honest?

173

Could I look every person I interviewed in the eye as the story aired, and each one would feel I was fair? Would my reporting, my behavior, and my motives make God smile or cringe?

174Increasingly, I hope to see my legacy as a pursuit of truth, but one soaked in kindness—I'd like to be remembered as a journalist who stayed "soft at the center" and still has been willing to report on the "foe in ambush." So often I am reminded that we work for eternal rewards; therefore, toiling anonymously, refraining from harming someone's reputation with "titillating" information when the other news outlets are piling on, bringing insight to important issues—the kind of work that receives no credit here on earth receives its rewards in heaven. And I hope to help young journalists see that they do not need to mortgage their soul for a story.

Points to Ponder

1. How do you desire for others to remember you?

2. Do you like how your story is unfolding?

3. Is embracing Christ's story the greatest longing of your heart?

FAITH

1. Henri Nouwen, *The Living Reminder* (Harper Collins, San Francisco, CA: 1977) p. 66.
2. Dotson Radar, "I Found Purpose," *Parade* magazine, July 7, 2002, p. 5
3. http://www.nd.edu/Departments/Maritain/ti01/gahl.htm#N_3_, accessed November 19, 2004.
4. Robert Coles, *The Call of Stories: Teaching and the Moral Imagination* (Houghton Mifflin, Boston, MA: 1989) p. 7.
5. Staff reports, "Voice of Cards Dies: He was the Soul of City," *St. Louis Post-Dispatch*, June 19, 2002, front page.

Adventures in Holy Matrimony
For Better or the Absolute Worst

Julie Anne Fidler

The Gutter
Where Life Is Meant to Be Lived

Craig Gross

Friendlationships
From Like, to Like Like, to Love in Your Twenties

Jeff Taylor

The Naked Christian
Taking Off Religion to Find True Relationship

Craig Borlase

**For more information on these titles
and more, check out**
www.relevantbooks.com

DON'T FORGET YOUR FREE SUBSCRIPTION TO RELEVANT

⌐ *TO REDEEM YOUR **FREE** 1/2 YEAR SUBSCRIPTION, SIMPLY GO TO*
www.relevantmagazine.com/~perspectives

Offer valid in the U.S. only. Please allow 6-8 weeks for delivery.

EACH ISSUE OF RELEVANT COVERS GOD, LIFE AND PROGRESSIVE CULTURE. YOU'LL FIND ARTICLES COVERING:

↗ God, church and how we can impact the world around us

↗ Life in your 20s—money, jobs, relationships and more

↗ The music, movies, TV and books that shape our culture

Created by twentysomethings for twentysomethings, RELEVANT is the only magazine of its kind. But don't take our word for it—sign up for your free 1/2 year subscription today!

YOU MAY ALSO BE INTERESTED IN...

God's Echo: Exploring
~~idrash~~
~~berg~~ Sasso

~~~3-8~~
~~~dcover~~

~~ed~~ that the Torah
~~l~~ therefore
~~truths~~ whose
~~tion.~~ In this
~~h~~ originated
~~slations~~ and
~~ash~~ texts.

~~angled~~
~~nd~~ Parables

~~translated~~
~~result~~ of a
~~aith~~ between
~~man~~ Catholic
~~is'~~ pithy
~~ly~~ simple,

Available from most booksellers or through Paraclete Press
www.paracletepress.com • 1-800-451-5006.
Try your local bookstore first.

ALSO BY PETER ROLLINS

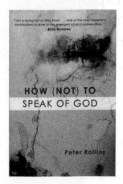

How (Not) to Speak of God

ISBN: 978-1-55725-505-1
$19.95, 192 pages
Paperback

How (Not) to Speak of God sets out to explore the philosophical/theological theory and praxis of the contemporary expression of emerging faith. Offering a rare international perspective, Rollins not only offers a clear exploration of this embryonic movement, but also provides key resources for those actively involved in developing emerging communities around the world.

"Here in pregnant bud is the rose, the emerging new configuration, of a Christianity that is neither Roman nor Protestant, neither Eastern nor monastic; but rather is the re-formation of all of them. Here, in pregnant bud, is third millennium Christendom."
—**Phyllis Tickle**

"Reading [*How (Not) to Speak of God*] did good for my mind and for my soul. . . . In fact, I would say this is one of the two or three most rewarding books of theology I have read in ten years."
—**Brian McLaren** *from the Foreword*